12 -

· Coating

Sweet Success

Sweet Success

STEVEN WHEELER

Photographs by Alan Newnham

ZACHARY KWINTNER BOOKS LTD.

First published in Great Britain in 1990 by
Anaya Publishers Limited
Strode House, 44–50 Osnaburgh Street, London NW1 3ND

This 1992 edition published by
Zachary Kwintner Books Ltd,
6/7 Warren Mews, London W1P 5DJ

Managing editor: Janet Illsley
Photographer: Alan Newnham
Designer: Harry Green
Editor: Norma Macmillan
Food stylist: Carole Handslip
Recipe techniques: Mandy Wagstaff
Photographic stylist: Maria Jacques
Calligrapher: Susanne Haines

ISBN 1 873734 02 6

Typeset in Great Britain by Tradespools Ltd, Frome, Somerset

Colour reproduction by Columbia Offset, Singapore

Printed and bound in Portugal by
Resopal Industria Grafica Lda

CONTENTS

◆

INTRODUCTION

＊

Illustrated with magnificent colour photographs, *Sweet Success* aims to be both practical and inspirational, and is planned to appeal to beginners and experienced cooks alike. It is divided into nine chapters and ranges from basic meringues to sponges, custards and elaborate pastry confections. Each section begins with a Master Recipe which tells you, step-by-step, how to make a basic preparation. Each Master Recipe is accompanied by a series of what I have called "watchpoints" to help you on your way.

If you are a beginner when it comes to making desserts, you can become totally familiar with a basic technique. You will then acquire the confidence to tackle other more complex recipes and, if you are ever unsure of a technique, you can always refer back to the watchpoint panels alongside every Master Recipe to ensure complete success every time. Those already familiar with all the basic cookery techniques can, of course, skip the step-by-step pages and use the book as a source of ideas for making fabulous international desserts.

Unlike many books on the subject, my aim in writing *Sweet Success* has been to help the reader establish a working knowledge of dessert making and the techniques involved. Experienced cooks will say that cooking is easy, and that while they may follow the occasional recipe, most of the time they make it up as they go along. (This sort of talk is hardly encouraging for those who can barely manage a lump-free custard.) What is it, then, that makes cooking so easy? When I set out to write this book, I asked myself the same question. Admittedly, I did serve a four-year apprenticeship in London and finished up working in Switzerland as a pastry cook, so I might be expected to have a few answers. Cooking is a bit like riding a bicycle: you don't necessarily think about what you are doing, you just get on with it. So, although the answers were in my head, they did take some sorting out. Without realising, for years I had based my understanding of desserts on a simple premise: every recipe I knew was based on one of nine basic preparations; this is how the structure of the book evolved.

My own fascination for desserts began in early childhood as I sat quietly in a corner of the kitchen watching my mother seemingly effortlessly prepare soft, gooey meringues, delicate cakes and custards and perfect ice creams. I made futile efforts to understand the mysteries that lay behind the wonderful aromas as her cakes and pastries emerged from the oven. Children, it seems to me now, were made for desserts and anyone who believes that kids simply demolish them without appreciating the work involved cannot know what it is to be loved and to have parents who spend time in the kitchen preparing food for them. Children are like elephants, they never forget.

This book, then, is written for everyone who like me remembers watching fascinated as their mother cooked, greedily licking spoons when she wasn't looking.

Blackcurrant Granita; Lemon Sorbet; Orange Sorbet.

'In cooking, as in all arts, simplicity is the sign of perfection'

CURNONSKY

One of the most useful, and many would say delicious, preparations at the disposal of the pastry cook is the basic meringue. So popular is its use in dessert-making that any dessert that contains meringue in one form or another is bound to be a great success. The most valuable asset of meringue is its ability to retain air, an essential property for soft mousses and smooth creams. When folded into flavoured crème pâtissière, the mixture will rise into an impressive soufflé. Another less common but equally delicious way with meringue is to poach it by floating shapes on hot liquid until set. Alternatively, meringue can be piled in a mould, baked in a *bain marie*, turned out and served with an appropriate sauce. Dried meringue shells or other shapes are always useful in the kitchen, not least for their keeping qualities which make them ideal for creating last-minute desserts. Soft fruits, spirits and liqueurs can be added to meringue to provide additional flavour.

Meringue-making is rarely without its problems. Even with years of experience, I still come across the occasional difficulty. The trick is not to despair but to seek explanation so that you can gain courage to try again. Over time I have encountered various remedies for meringue failures, many of which I have discarded as pure twaddle, but what remains is a collection of useful antidotes. The symptoms that we are all familiar with include reluctant drying, beads of moisture, weepy bottoms, chewy centres, browning and sticking to the paper. I will show you how to deal with these and others in this section.

Crisp, light Meringue to an irresistible vacherin of berry fruits

Successful Meringue

Approaching the subject of meringue we are faced with two simple ingredients – egg whites and caster sugar. By adjusting the amounts of sugar to egg white we can vary the density of the meringue according to its use. If we whisk plain egg whites without any sugar at all they will gain volume quickly but will separate easily, thus losing their smoothness. As we add sugar we notice that the meringue gains stability as well as smoothness, making it easy to combine with other ingredients.

The first rule for successful meringue is to ensure perfect cleanliness. The importance of this cannot be overstated since any trace of grease found on or in the equipment and ingredients will prevent the meringue from gaining volume. Mixing bowls are best made of stainless steel, copper or glass and should be cleaned with hot soapy water, rinsed well and dried before use. Soft plastic bowls are prone to harbouring grease so should be avoided. One of the most common faults when making meringue is the contamination of egg whites with egg yolk; traces of stray egg yolk can be removed successfully using a broken egg shell. Open packets of sugar often contain particles of flour or other debris which will in turn prevent the meringue from whisking properly. It is therefore best to open a new packet of sugar when making meringue.

The second rule is to use egg whites at room temperature. If the whites are used straight from the fridge, the cold air in them will contract as they are being whisked, thus preventing the meringue from gaining sufficient volume.

The third rule concerns the method used and the choice of equipment. I choose to whisk egg whites by hand, not for the sake of martyrdom but because I find it a bother to search for, plug in and afterwards clean an electric mixer and its accessories. The hard work associated with hand whisking can be minimized by ensuring that the bowl is held at just below waist level. Resting the bowl on a kitchen stool or in an open drawer should put it at the right height.

Another labour-saving piece of advice concerns the speed at which the egg whites are whisked. There is little profit in whisking at high speed since this has a tendency to knock the air out of the meringue as well as the strength out of your arm very quickly. Hand whisking is a casual affair that relies on efficiency rather than strength. If, after all this soft talk, you prefer to use an electric mixer, note that low speeds will produce a better meringue.

Illustrated overleaf: Blueberry Meringue Tart; Vacherin of Soft Berry Fruits; Oeufs à la Neige.

1

Choose a dry day. Meringues will not turn out well when the weather is damp or humid.

2

Make sure you are familiar with the recipe and weigh ingredients carefully before you begin.

3

The worst enemy of meringue is grease. Egg whites must therefore be free from any trace of egg yolk, and equipment and utensils must be washed thoroughly with hot soapy water, rinsed well and dried before use.

4

If you are using a machine for whisking, make sure it is perfectly clean. Bits of flour and other debris can easily fall into the meringue and they will prevent it from gaining volume.

5

Soft plastic bowls are inclined to harbour grease and are best avoided.

6

Stray egg yolk is easily removed from egg white with a half shell.

7

Caster is the best sugar to use for meringues. To be sure the sugar is free of all traces of flour and other debris, use a fresh packet.

8

Cream of tartar, lemon juice, salt and other additives are not necessary for making meringues, providing your egg whites and sugar are clean.

9

Egg whites should be used at room temperature.

10

It is important to realize that meringues are dried rather than baked. Ovens, therefore, must be adequately ventilated.

11

Insufficient ventilation will cause meringues to steam, soften and become spongy.

12

If the oven temperature is too low, the meringues will tend to shrink and become hard.

13

If the oven temperature is too high, the meringues will tend to soufflé and brown, leaving the inside hard and chewy.

14

If you think your oven requires additional ventilation try wedging the door open slightly with a folded tea towel. Don't overdo it, though — too much ventilation can cause oven temperature to fall.

The first mistake that many cooks make when attempting meringue for the first time is to suppose that meringues are baked. In fact, they are dried, and the drying must be done in a well-ventilated oven. Egg whites contain 86% water, and this moisture must be allowed to evaporate effectively to ensure a dry crisp result. With insufficient oven ventilation, the meringues will in effect steam rather than dry, and beads of moisture will form on the surface. The finished texture will probably be akin to a soft sticky mess. If your oven is poorly ventilated, and most seem to be these days, hold the oven door open 1 cm/½ inch or so with a folded tea towel. In this way it won't lose any heat.

If the oven is not hot enough, the meringues will tend to shrink and become hard. Too hot an oven will cause the sugar to caramelize, resulting in meringues with a chewy toffee centre. Some people prefer their meringues like this although they tend to bring to a halt any conversation at the dinner table.

The best tray for drying meringues is a thin wooden board (your timber merchant can cut a piece to fit your oven). Metal baking sheets and trays have a tendency to conduct too much heat and often produce weepy-bottomed meringues. If you are unable to

Meringue Shells

obtain a wooden board, line metal trays with 3–4 layers of newspaper. Non-stick baking parchment is the best surface on which to dry the meringues, although greaseproof paper brushed with melted butter or oil and lightly dusted with flour will work just as well.

MAKES 36 SHELLS
4 egg whites, at room temperature
225 g/8 oz caster sugar

1 Preheat the oven to 140°C/ 275°F/gas 1 and line two thin wooden boards with non stick baking parchment. Alternatively, line two metal baking sheets or trays with newspaper followed by parchment. Put to one side.

2 Separate the egg whites into a perfectly clean stainless steel,

glass or copper mixing bowl, ensuring there is no trace of egg yolk. Whisk the egg whites steadily until they will hold their weight on the whisk. Add the sugar a little at a time, continuing to whisk until the meringue is stiff and shiny.

3 Without delay, spoon the meringue into a large piping bag fitted with a plain or star-shaped

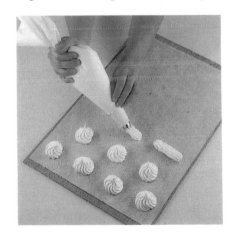

nozzle and pipe into regular shapes on the paper-lined baking trays. Alternatively, the meringue can be spooned onto the trays.

4 For a special effect, sprinkle the meringues with caster sugar, crushed praline or cocoa powder. Put the trays into the preheated oven and dry for 15 minutes, holding the door slightly ajar if necessary for

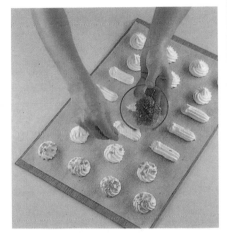

ventilation. After this time, reduce the temperature to 120°C/250°F/ gas ½ and allow the meringues to dry completely for 2-3 hours. Allow to cool, then remove from the paper and transfer the meringues to an airtight jar or tin where they will keep for 1–2 months.

VARIATIONS
Hazelnut Meringues: Stir 50 g/2 oz ground roasted hazelnuts into the meringue mixture before piping or shaping.

Chocolate Meringues: Sift 2 tbsp cocoa powder over the meringue mixture and fold in evenly. Pipe or shape as required.

Coconut Meringues: Fold 50 g/2 oz desiccated coconut into the meringue and spoon into heaps on the baking trays. After drying, dip into melted chocolate.

Oeufs à la Neige

SERVES 4–6

575 ml/1 pint milk

4 eggs, at room temperature

150 g/5 oz caster sugar

½ vanilla pod, or 3 drops of vanilla
   essence

2 tbsp cornflour

2 tbsp cold milk or water

Caramel:

150 g/5 oz caster sugar

Oeufs à la Neige, Snow Eggs or Floating Islands as they are often called, are lightly poached meringue ovals floating on a vanilla-scented custard and topped with a rich, dark caramel. This is a classical dessert that features in many of the finest restaurants. It is designed for guests who have over-indulged on their main course and require a sweet little nothing to smooth the palate before coffee.

———————— ◆ ————————

Pour the milk into a large shallow saucepan and bring to a simmer. Separate the egg whites into a clean mixing bowl; put the yolks in another bowl. Whisk the egg whites until they will hold their own weight on the whisk. Add 75 g/3 oz of the sugar a little at a time, and continue whisking until stiff peaks form.

Shape the meringue into ovals between two tablespoons dipped in warm water, and float the shapes on the simmering milk. Poach gently for 2 minutes, turning once; do not allow the milk to boil rapidly or the meringues will tend to soufflé and lose their shape. Carefully lift the meringues, which will be soft but firm to touch, out of the milk and place on a tray lined with a damp tea towel.

To prepare the vanilla custard, split the vanilla pod open to reveal the tiny black seeds and add to the hot poaching milk, or add the vanilla essence. Add the remaining caster sugar and the cornflour to the egg yolks with the cold milk or water and stir until smooth. Pour the poaching milk over the egg yolk mixture and stir to mix, then pour into a smaller heavy saucepan. Stir the custard to the boil and simmer briefly to thicken. Strain the custard into a serving bowl and allow to cool to room temperature, then float the meringues on top.

To prepare the caramel, measure 2 tbsp of the sugar into a small heavy saucepan and melt over a moderate heat until liquid but not brown. Add a further 2 tbsp of the sugar and stir until dissolved. Continue to add the sugar in this way, then allow to caramelize to a deep mahogany brown. Without delay, spoon the caramel over the white meringues.

Oeufs à la Neige can be made up to 3 hours before serving, and are best eaten the same day.

Illustrated on page 11

Vacherin of Soft Berry Fruits

SERVES 6–8

5 egg whites, at room temperature

225 g/8 oz caster sugar

150 g/5 oz icing sugar

Filling:

425 ml/15 fl oz double cream

3 tbsp caster sugar

2 tbsp dry sherry, Kirsch or Grand Marnier

350 g/12 oz fresh or frozen mixed raspberries, blackberries, redcurrants and strawberries

To finish:

cluster of fresh redcurrants and blackcurrants, or 15 g/$\frac{1}{2}$ oz crystallized violets or rose petals

The vacherin is known amongst French pastry buffs as the European version of the Australian Pavlova. The difference is that the Pavlova has a deep, soft meringue base, whereas the vacherin has a crisp case. Both are filled with a mixture of fresh fruit and cream. The vacherin has the advantage that it can be made well in advance and stored in an airtight container ready for use.

———— ◆ ————

Preheat the oven to 140°C/275°F/gas 1. Line two wooden baking trays with non-stick baking parchment (see page 12). Draw a 23 cm/9 inch circle on one of the baking trays, using a plate of the same size as a guide. Set aside.

Whisk 4 of the egg whites in a clean mixing bowl until they will hold their weight on the whisk. Add the caster sugar a little at a time, continuing to whisk until stiff and shiny. Spoon the meringue into a large piping bag fitted with a large plain nozzle.

Pipe the meringue in a continuous spiral within the marked circle, starting in the centre. Pipe the remainder of the meringue into twenty 6 cm/2$\frac{1}{2}$ inch oval shells on the other baking tray. Dry the meringues in the preheated oven for 15 minutes, then reduce the temperature of the oven to 120°C/250°F/gas $\frac{1}{2}$ and leave the meringues to dry in the oven for a further 2–3 hours. Allow to cool completely.

To assemble the vacherin case, put the remaining egg white into a mixing bowl and stir in the icing sugar. Use to secure 12 meringue shells around the edge of the meringue base, overlapping them slightly.

To prepare the filling, loosely whip the cream with the caster sugar and flavour with sherry, Kirsch or Grand Marnier, according to taste. Break up the remaining meringue shells and fold into the cream. Turn into the centre of the meringue case. Scatter the soft fruits over the cream and decorate with clusters of fresh currants, crystallized violets or rose petals, as desired. Serve within 1 hour of assembling.

Illustrated on page 10

VARIATION

Tropical Fruit Vacherin: Fold 25 g/1 oz desiccated coconut into the meringue mixture. Dip the meringue shells in melted chocolate and assemble the case. Flavour filling with rum and top with tropical fruits – mango, kiwi fruit, pineapple, banana, paw paw or papaya, and passion fruit.

Meringue Bombe Jewelled with Ruby Fruits

SERVES 4

soft butter for greasing

50 g/2 oz flaked almonds, toasted

4 egg whites, at room temperature

125 g/4 oz caster sugar

225 g/8 oz mixed berry fruits, fresh or frozen, such as strawberries, raspberries, redcurrants, blackcurrants, blackberries

3/4 recipe Egg Custard Sauce (page 39), cooled

Preheat the oven to 180°C/350°F/gas 4. Lightly grease an 18 cm/7 inch soufflé dish or a 1.1 litre/2 pint bombe mould with the soft butter, cover base and sides with toasted almonds and put to one side.

Separate the egg whites into a clean mixing bowl and whisk until they will hold their weight on the whisk, then add the sugar a little at a time and continue whisking until stiff. Fold in the chosen fruit, and turn into the prepared mould.

Stand the mould in a roasting pan, half fill the pan with boiling water and bake in the preheated oven for 25 minutes. Allow the bombe to cool a little before turning out on to a serving dish. Serve with the custard.

Fresh Fruit Pavlova

SERVES 6–8

4 egg whites, at room temperature

225 g/8 oz caster sugar

1 tsp white wine vinegar

1 tsp cornflour

Filling:

275 ml/10 fl oz double cream

2 tbsp caster sugar

2 tbsp eau-de-vie de Framboise, Kirsch or dry sherry

450 g/1 lb raspberries, fresh or frozen, or other berry fruits

50 g/2 oz flaked almonds, toasted

icing sugar for sprinkling

Brittle on the outside, internally soft, Pavlovas belong to the season of soft berry fruits which can be seen at their best nestling in cream and meringue.

———— ◆ ————

Preheat the oven to 140°/275°F/gas 1. Line a wooden baking tray with non-stick baking parchment and mark on it a 20 cm/8 inch circle. (see page 12). Set aside.

Place the egg whites in a clean mixing bowl and whisk until they will hold their weight on the whisk. Add the sugar a little at a time, continuing to whisk until stiff and shiny. Add the wine vinegar and cornflour and stir briefly.

Spread the meringue on the drawn circle to cover. Transfer to the preheated oven and bake for 2 hours. Allow to cool completely.

To prepare the filling, loosely whip the cream with the sugar and flavour with the liqueur or sherry.

To assemble the Pavlova, spread half of the cream over the meringue base and pile on half of the raspberries. Cover with the remaining cream and raspberries followed by a sprinkling of toasted flaked almonds and icing sugar. Once assembled, Pavlovas are best eaten within 3–4 hours.

Meringue Bombe Jewelled with Ruby Fruits; Fresh Fruit Pavlova.

Flaming Igloos

SERVES 4

one 20 cm/8 inch plain whisked
 sponge (page 119)
1 small fresh pineapple, peeled,
 cored and cut into rings, or
 200 g/7 oz canned pineapple rings
 in syrup
2 tbsp Kirsch or Grand Marnier
4 scoops strawberry ice cream or
 sorbet
3 egg whites, at room temperature
125 g/4 oz caster sugar

Syrup (optional):

3 tbsp caster sugar
150 ml/5 fl oz boiling water

A sense of humour is one of the most important ingredients for the adventurous cook. Flaming Igloos is one dessert that will bring a touch of light relief towards the end of the meal.

———— ◆ ————

Slice the sponge into three layers using a long serrated knife. Cut out four 7.5 cm/3 inch rounds with a plain biscuit cutter.

If using fresh pineapple, make a syrup by dissolving the caster sugar in the boiling water. For canned pineapple, use the syrup from the can.

Moisten the sponge rounds with the syrup and sprinkle each with Kirsch or Grand Marnier. Place a pineapple ring on each round and top each with a scoop of strawberry ice cream or sorbet. Cover the exposed ice cream with thin slices of the remaining sponge and transfer to the freezer.

To make the meringue, whisk the egg whites in a clean mixing bowl until they will hold their weight on the whisk. Add the sugar a little at a time and continue whisking until stiff.

Spread the meringue liberally over the Igloo shapes. Return to the freezer for up to 1 hour – no longer or the pineapple is likely to freeze solid.

To finish, preheat the oven to 230°C/450°F/gas 8. Bake the Igloos for 2–3 minutes near top of oven until golden brown. Serve immediately.

Illustrated on page 21

Blueberry Meringue Tart

SERVES 6

350 g/12 oz sweet shortcrust pastry
 (page 137)
3 egg whites, at room temperature
125 g/4 oz caster sugar
225 g/8 oz blueberries
extra caster sugar for sprinkling

Fluffy white meringue becomes the perfect vehicle for soft summer fruits in a crisp pastry case. By flashing the tart under a hot grill, the meringue filling will become firm enough to cut into neat slices. This tart is also delicious made with redcurrants, passion fruit, raspberries or blackberries.

———— ◆ ————

Roll out the pastry on a lightly floured work surface to a thickness of 3 mm/$\frac{1}{8}$ inch and use to line a 20 cm/8 inch flan tin (see page 140). Leave to rest in the refrigerator for 1 hour.

Preheat the oven to 200°C/400°F/gas 6. Line a 20 cm/8 inch flan case with greaseproof paper, fill with baking beans and bake blind in the centre of the preheated oven for 25–30 minutes. Remove paper and beans and allow to cool.

To prepare the filling, whisk the egg whites in a clean bowl until they will hold their weight on the whisk. Add the sugar a little at a time and continue whisking until stiff. Fold in the berries and turn into the flan case. Sprinkle with extra caster sugar and place under a preheated medium grill for 1–2 minutes until browned. After grilling the meringue becomes quite firm and will hold its shape for up to 8 hours.

Illustrated on page 10

Baked Alaska Eskimo Joe

WATCHPOINTS
◆
Meringue ◆ Whisked Sponge

SERVES 4–6
one 20 cm/8 inch plain whisked
    sponge (page 119)
500 ml/18 fl oz (¹/₂ recipe) vanilla ice
    cream (page 53)
500 ml/18 fl oz (¹/₂ recipe) chocolate
    ice cream (page 53)
1–2 × 200 g/7 oz cans stoned black
    cherries, well drained
2 tbsp Kirsch or brandy
4 egg whites, at room temperature
150 g/5 oz caster sugar

A lot of fun can be had with Baked Alaskas, not least because of the variety of fillings that can be put inside them. During my apprenticeship in French-speaking Switzerland, it was one of the chef's birthdays. As a surprise, we decorated a balloon with meringue to look like a Baked Alaska. After considerable pomp and ceremony, the delighted chef was given a pointed knife with which to cut into the monstrosity. Which fell quicker, the 'dessert' or the look on his face, I don't remember!

———— ◆ ————

Slice the sponge into three layers. Line a 30 cm/12 inch long ovenproof oval plate with pieces of sponge. Cut the ice cream into large slivers. Working quickly, overlap upright slivers of ice cream on the sponge to form an oval well. If you are delayed, return it to the freezer. Place the cherries in the well and sprinkle with Kirsch or brandy. Mould the ice cream over the cherries to enclose them, then cover the ice cream with a layer of sponge. Place in the freezer whilst you prepare the meringue.

Whisk the egg whites in a clean mixing bowl until they will hold their weight on the whisk. Add the sugar a little at a time and continue whisking until stiff. Cover the Alaska with the meringue, using a palette knife or spatula. If planning ahead, the Alaska can be kept in the freezer for up to 2 hours before the cherries begin to freeze.

To finish, preheat the oven to 220°C/425°F/gas 7. Bake the Alaska for 10 minutes, or until golden brown. Serve immediately.

Chocolate and Hazelnut Meringue Layer Gâteau

SERVES 4–6

50 g/2 oz shelled hazelnuts

4 egg whites, at room temperature

225 g/8 oz caster sugar

1 tbsp cocoa powder

¹/₂ tsp ground cinnamon

Filling:

275 ml/10 fl oz double cream

2 tbsp caster sugar

To finish:

125 g/4 oz plain chocolate in a block

icing sugar for dusting (optional)

Hazelnuts have a particular affinity with meringue and are further enhanced in this delicious recipe by the addition of cocoa powder and ground cinnamon. On a warm day, you will need to refrigerate the flaked or grated chocolate before handling.

———— ◆ ————

Preheat the oven to 140°C/275°F/gas 1. Line two wooden baking trays with non-stick baking parchment (see master recipe). Draw three 18 cm/7 inch circles on the paper and put to one side.

Grind the hazelnuts in a coffee mill or food processor until fine. Spread out the nuts on a baking sheet and toast them under a hot grill to bring out their full flavour.

To prepare the meringue, whisk the egg whites in a clean mixing bowl until they will hold their weight on the whisk. Add the sugar a little at a time and continue whisking until stiff. Sieve the ground hazelnuts, cocoa and cinnamon over the meringue and fold in with a spatula.

Divide the meringue between the three marked circles and spread out evenly. Dry the meringues in the preheated oven for 15 minutes, then reduce the temperature to 120°C/250°F/gas ¹/₂ and dry for a further 2–3 hours. Allow to cool completely.

To assemble the gâteau, loosely whip the cream with the sugar and use to sandwich the meringue layers together, saving enough cream for the top. To finish, flake the chocolate by scraping it with a metal biscuit cutter or the curved blade of a palette knife onto a sheet of greaseproof paper. Alternatively, grate the chocolate coarsely on a cheese grater. Decorate the top of the gâteau with chocolate flakes and dust with icing sugar if desired.

VARIATION

Raspberry and Hazelnut Meringue Gâteau: Omit the cocoa powder and cinnamon from the meringue. Fold 125 g/4 oz lightly crushed raspberries into two thirds of the cream filling before assembling the gâteau. Decorate the top with the remaining cream and fresh raspberries.

Chocolate and Hazelnut Meringue Layer Gâteau; Flaming Igloos (page 18).

Crème pâtissière, or confectioner's custard, is to the confectioner what a basic white sauce is to the sauce cook. Both preparations offer similar qualities of smoothness and both are indispensable for the creation of new and exciting dishes. The French have been responsible for the refinement of crème pâtissière as we know it today and have done much to promote its success worldwide. Wherever French cooking is taught, one of the first lessons learned is how to make a good crème pâtissière.

Its preparation couldn't be more straightforward, nor the ingredients — eggs, flour, sugar and milk — simpler. The eggs, flour and sugar are combined together with a little of the milk until smooth. The remaining milk is brought to the boil, combined with the egg mixture and returned to the heat to thicken.

Flavoured with fruit purée, chocolate or liqueur and lightened with whisked egg white, crème pâtissière becomes a hot soufflé. Blended with whipped cream and flavoured with a liqueur, crème pâtissière is turned into a delicious filling for fruit flans, tarts, roulades, éclairs and profiteroles.

Travel south through France, past cream-producing Normandy and Île de France, and you will notice that as the weather becomes warmer, less and less cream is used in the making of cakes and pastries because, of course, cream would spoil in the heat. The French have not surprisingly come up with a delicious solution to this problem — simply a mixture of whipped cream and crème pâtissière known as crème diplomat. It can be used whenever whipped cream will not stand up to the heat of the day.

Arguably one of the smoothest and most satisfying derivatives of crème pâtissière is crème chiboust — featured in many French cakes and pastries. It was invented one day when someone, wondering what to do with the egg

Crème Pâtissière

Classic French confection

whites left over from making crème pâtissière, decided to whisk them into a soft meringue and fold them into the hot crème pâtissière. The heat of the crème pâtissière causes the meringue to set slightly, making a deliciously smooth cream. Crème chiboust is an ideal filling for fresh fruit tarts, flans and whisked sponges.

In France children and adults have a special affection for crème pâtissière and it would seem that if they are not talking about it, they are eating it. If they are doing neither they are probably asleep dreaming about it. According to one lady I once met in Tours, crème pâtissière plays an important part in French life and I am told holds one of the secrets of eternal youth. Apparently we are only young for as long as we can retain our passion for crème pâtissière. This I am assured is easily done since crème pâtissière is used in so many delicious desserts and pastries that it would be difficult not to eat it. This lady of Tours was, I might add, a trifle overweight, so do mind how you go!

Hot Soufflé

A bowl of crème pâtissière, five eggs and twenty minutes in a hot oven are the makings of a fabulous hot soufflé, which will do wonders for your reputation as an accomplished cook.

If, however, you are one of the many who cannot get a soufflé to rise – or stay risen for long enough to breathe a sigh of relief – the fault may lie in over-simplified recipe instructions. Missing details could make the difference between success and failure.

The three most important lessons to learn in soufflé-making are preparing the dish properly, knowing the correct consistency of the crème pâtissière, and checking the smoothness of the meringue before folding in.

Soufflé flavourings can be almost as varied as the cook's imagination. Soft berry fruits lend themselves particularly well, for their sharp flavour and attractive colour. Citrus fruits are equally popular. Try folding liqueur-soaked pieces of macaroon into a soufflé mixture before baking.

Chocolate is a popular flavouring, but few other ingredients cause as many problems when it comes to soufflé-making. The oils and cocoa butter in block chocolate prevent the soufflé from rising, usually resulting in a foaming soup. Chocolate soufflés are therefore best made with cocoa powder, with perhaps a splash of Crème de Cacao or dark rum to liven up the occasion.

Illustrated overleaf: Continental Fruit Tart; berry fruits topped with Crème Diplomat; Puits d'Amour.

to an impressive hot soufflé

1

Make sure that you are familiar with the recipe and measure all ingredients carefully before commencing.

2

Free-range eggs give a brighter colour and richer flavour to crème pâtissière.

3

Choose a heavy saucepan and a wooden spoon that will reach into the corners of the pan as you stir the crème pâtissière. To prevent the milk from catching, first rinse the saucepan out with cold water.

4

To avoid lumpy crème pâtissière, ensure that the flour, egg and sugar mixture is perfectly smooth before incorporating the hot milk.

5

Always taste crème pâtissière before cooling to ensure it is sufficiently cooked. Undercooked crème pâtissière tastes of raw flour.

6

Cover the surface of crème pâtissière closely with a butter paper or a piece of buttered greaseproof paper to prevent a skin forming as the crème pâtissière cools.

WHIPPING • CREAM

Ensure the cream is cold before whipping.

◆

If whisking with an electric mixer, use a low or medium speed to give you more control.

◆

Properly whipped cream should be of a dropping consistency.

As cream is handled, ie. spread, piped or stirred, it continues to whip and can easily lose its smoothness.

◆

If cream appears to be off-white when whipped, it is not cold enough and will over-whip very easily.

Perhaps the saddest moment for any cook is when he or she walks into the kitchen and discovers that there is nothing there to inspire them. But provide them with a bowl of smooth crème pâtissière and they will create some of the most delicious desserts you can imagine.

MAKES 425 ml/15 fl oz
350 ml/12 fl oz milk
1/2 vanilla pod, split open, or 1/2 tsp vanilla essence
6 egg yolks
50 g/2 oz caster sugar
25 g/1 oz plain flour

1 Measure 4 tbsp of the milk into a mixing bowl. Put the remainder of the milk in a heavy saucepan that has been rinsed out with cold water. Add the vanilla pod or essence and bring to the boil. Add the egg yolks, sugar and flour to the

milk in the mixing bowl and stir together with a hand whisk until smooth.

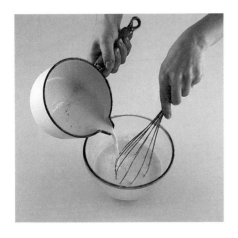

2 When the milk in the pan has come to the boil, pour it over the egg mixture and stir until evenly mixed. Although the crème pâtissière will thicken slightly from the heat of the milk, it must be returned to the saucepan and gently simmered for 3–4 minutes, stirring constantly, to cook the flour. Remove from the heat and discard the vanilla pod.

3 Pour the crème pâtissière into a bowl and cover the surface with a butter paper or a piece of buttered greaseproof paper. Allow to cool, and refrigerate before use. Well covered, crème pâtissière will keep in the refrigerator for up to

5 days. Use as a delicious filling for fruit flans, tarts, pastries, chocolate éclairs, etc.

VARIATIONS

Crème Diplomat: Prepare the crème pâtissière as above and allow to cool. Fold 150 ml/5 fl oz loosely whipped double cream into the cold crème pâtissière and chill until required. It will keep in the refrigerator for up to 48 hours. Use as a delicious alternative to whipped cream.

Praline Crème Pâtissière: Prepare the crème pâtissière as above and allow to cool, then stir in 75 g/3 oz crushed praline. Use as a filling for fruit flans and tartlets. This is particularly good when combined with cream to make Praline Crème Diplomat.

Chocolate Crème Pâtissière: Prepare the crème pâtissière as above and stir in 125 g/4 oz best quality plain chocolate in pieces until melted. Flavour as desired with dark rum, whisky or Kirsch and allow to cool. Use as a filling for chocolate cakes, éclairs and special tarts.

Almond Crème Pâtissière: Prepare the crème pâtissière as above, but omit sugar and dissolve 50 g/2 oz white marzipan in the hot milk before adding it to the egg mixture. Flavour with Amaretto or Kirsch;

then allow to cool. Use as a filling for apricot, cherry or plum tarts.

Crème Chiboust: Prepare the crème pâtissière as above, retaining three of the egg whites and omitting the sugar. Whisk the egg whites in a clean mixing bowl until they will

hold their weight on the whisk. Add 50 g/2 oz sugar a little at a time and continue whisking until soft peaks can be formed. While the custard is still simmering, fold in the soft meringue with a large metal spoon or spatula until even. Allow to cool before using.

Crème chiboust will keep in the refrigerator for up to 24 hours. Use as a delicious filling for fresh fruit tarts, flans and sponge cakes. Or fold in 2 sliced fresh peaches, 225 g/8 oz raspberries and 3–4 crushed macaroons. Serve, sprinkled with toasted flaked almonds as a dessert.

1

Soufflés will only rise in straight-sided dishes; proper soufflé dishes are preferable.

2

The higher the sides of the dish, the more the soufflé will rise.

3

Be generous when greasing a soufflé dish especially the sides. To ensure a good even coating, smear the butter around the inside of the soufflé dish, using two fingers of one hand.

4

Eggs are best used at room temperature. Free-range eggs make for a richer, more lively soufflé.

5

When whisking the egg whites, add a little sugar to help retain their smoothness.

6

Should the egg whites become grainy and lose their smoothness, let them stand for 2–3 minutes and whisk again.

7

The crème pâtissière base and the meringue must be of a similar consistency to ensure that they combine well together.

8

By folding the meringue into a *hot* custard base, the egg whites will set slightly thus preventing the mixture from collapsing.

9

Fill the soufflé dish with the mixture and smooth the surface so it is level with the rim of the dish.

10

The perfectly cooked soufflé has a slightly undercooked, creamy centre.

COMMON ◆ FAULTS

Not greasing the soufflé dish well enough with soft butter.

◆

Trying to fold beaten egg whites into a crème pâtissière that is too stiff.

◆

Using too few egg whites for the amount of crème pâtissière.

Flavouring the soufflé with oily ingredients such as block chocolate, bananas and nuts.

◆

Adding too much sugar to the whisked egg white (this will cause the soufflé to spill over the edge of the dish).

◆

Baking in too cool an oven.

This recipe can be adapted to make any number of variations. It is however best to try the master recipe before attempting others.

SERVES 4

25 g/1 oz soft butter for greasing
a little caster sugar for coating
225 ml/8 fl oz milk
4 eggs, at room temperature, separated
6 tbsp caster sugar
2 tbsp plain flour
finely grated zest and juice of 2 lemons
icing sugar to decorate

1 Preheat the oven to 200°C/400°F/gas 6. Liberally grease an 18 cm/7 inch soufflé dish with the soft butter, paying particular attention to the sides, and sprinkle with caster sugar to coat.

2 To make the crème pâtissière base, measure 2 tbsp of the milk into a mixing bowl. Bring the remainder of the milk to the boil in a saucepan. Add the egg yolks, 2 tbsp of the sugar and the flour to the milk in the mixing bowl and stir with a hand whisk until smooth. When the milk in the pan has come to the boil, pour it over the egg mixture and stir until even. Return the crème pâtissière to the saucepan, add the lemon zest and juice and simmer gently for 3–4 minutes, stirring constantly until thickened.

3 Whisk the egg whites in a clean mixing bowl until they will hold their weight on the whisk. Gradually add the remaining 4 tbsp sugar and continue whisking until soft peaks can be formed. The

meringue should be as smooth as the hot crème pâtissière. To ensure smoothness, it is best to give the meringue a final whisking by hand just before folding in. Remove the crème pâtissière from the heat and stir in a whisk-full of meringue until even. Fold in the remainder of the meringue with a large metal spoon or rubber spatula. At this stage the mixture should be thick enough to leave a finger trace across the back of the spoon.

4 Turn the mixture into the prepared dish and spread level with the top. Place the dish in the centre of the preheated oven and bake for 20–25 minutes. Dust with icing sugar and serve.

The perfectly cooked soufflé should still have a soft centre which acts as a light sauce.

VARIATIONS

Soufflé Grand Marnier: Proceed as for the basic soufflé, omitting lemon; add 4 macaroons, crumbled and soaked in 4 tbsp Grand Marnier, to the crème pâtissière.

Raspberry Soufflé: Proceed as for the basic soufflé, omitting lemon and adding 175 g/6 oz raspberries, puréed and sieved, to the crème pâtissière.

Strawberry Soufflé: Proceed as for the basic soufflé, omitting lemon and adding 175 g/6 oz strawberries, puréed, to the crème pâtissière.

Passion Fruit Soufflé: Proceed as for the basic soufflé, omitting lemon and adding the juice and flesh of 5 passion fruit to the crème pâtissière.

Chocolate Soufflé: Proceed as for the basic soufflé, omitting the lemon and adding 3 tbsp cocoa powder and 2 tbsp Crème de Cacao, dark rum or whisky to the crème pâtissière.

Mango and Raspberry Soufflé: Proceed as for basic soufflé, omitting the lemon. Flavour half crème pâtissière with 75 g/3 oz mango purée and 2 tbsp tequila, and the remainder with 75 g/3 oz raspberry purée. Fold half of the meringue into each mixture and spoon alternately into dish.

Continental Fruit Tart

WATCHPOINTS
◆
Pastry ◆ Crème Pâtissière

SERVES 6–8
1 recipe rich biscuit pastry (page 139), or sweet shortcrust pastry (page 137)
4 tbsp apricot or raspberry jam
1 tbsp water

Filling:
½ recipe crème pâtissière (page 27)
700 g/1½ lb seasonal fruits, such as strawberries, raspberries, blueberries, blackberries, peach slices, apricot halves and grapes

During the height of summer, when soft berry fruits are plentiful, it is well worth putting together a continental-style fruit tart filled with crème pâtissière. If you are preparing ahead, you can have the pastry case, filling and fruits ready for last-minute assembly.

———— ◆ ————

Preheat the oven to 200°C/400°F/gas 6. Roll out the rich biscuit or short-crust pastry and use to line a 23 cm/9 inch flan ring placed on a baking sheet, or a loose-based flan tin (see page 140). Line the flan case with greaseproof paper, fill with baking beans and bake blind for 30–35 minutes, then allow to cool completely.

Prepare the crème pâtissière and allow to cool. Spread an even layer of crème pâtissière in the pastry case and decorate with the fruit.

To glaze, place the jam in a small saucepan with the water and stir to the boil. Sieve the glaze and brush evenly over the fruit. Leave to cool and set. Serve the fruit tart at room temperature.

Illustrated on page 24

Puits d'Amour

WATCHPOINTS
◆
Crème Pâtissière ◆ Pastry

SERVES 4–6
1 recipe shortcrust pastry (page 137)
275 g/10 oz fresh strawberries, or 4 tbsp best strawberry jam
1 recipe crème chiboust (page 27)

Roughly translated, the title of this recipe means 'Well of Love', and there couldn't be a more appropriate name to describe a delicious strawberry tart hidden beneath a mountain of fluffy crème pâtissière.

———— ◆ ————

Roll out the pastry on a lightly floured work surface to a thickness of 3 mm/⅛ inch and use to line a 23 cm/9 inch flan ring placed on a baking sheet, or a loose-based flan tin (see page 140). Trim the edges and leave to rest in the refrigerator for 1 hour.

Preheat the oven to 190°C/375°F/gas 5. Line the flan case with grease-proof paper, fill with baking beans and bake blind for 25–30 minutes. Allow to cool completely.

Hull the strawberries, cut into quarters and scatter two thirds of them into the flan case. If using jam instead of strawberries, spread over the base of the flan case using the back of a tablespoon. Pile the crème chiboust into the flan case and decorate the top with the remaining strawberries. Serve immediately.

Illustrated on page 25

VARIATION
If other soft berry fruits are in season, why not try combinations of raspberries, redcurrants, blackberries and blueberries.

Crème Pâtissière Fritters with an Apricot Sauce

WATCHPOINTS
◆
Crème Pâtissière ◆ Meringue
———————— ◆ ————————

SERVES 4–6
soft butter for greasing
1 recipe crème pâtissière (page 27)
200 g/7 oz canned apricot halves in syrup
few drops of Kirsch or Amaretto
vegetable oil for deep frying
plain flour for dusting
icing sugar for dusting

Batter:
75 g/3 oz plain flour
150 ml/¼ pint milk
2 eggs, at room temperature, separated
2 tbsp caster sugar

For the uninitiated, the idea of frying custard may seem a little odd, but when pieces of firm crème pâtissière are dipped into a fluffy batter, fried into golden nuggets, dusted with icing sugar and served with an apricot sauce, the initiation could well become an obsession.

———————— ◆ ————————

Lightly grease a large soup plate with butter and put to one side. Prepare the crème pâtissière, pour into the soup plate and leave to cool and set.

To prepare a simple apricot sauce, place the apricots together with their syrup in a food processor or blender and whizz into a smooth purée. Add a few drops of Kirsch or Amaretto to improve the flavour. Set aside.

To prepare the batter, measure the flour into a mixing bowl, make a well in the centre, pour in half of the milk and stir to a thick, even batter. Add the remainder of the milk and the egg yolks and stir until smooth. Just before making the fritters, whisk the egg whites until they will hold their weight on the whisk, then gradually add the sugar and continue whisking until the meringue will form soft peaks. Fold in the batter.

Heat the frying oil to 196°C/385°F. Turn the firm crème pâtissière on to a sheet of greaseproof paper and cut into 2.5 cm/1 inch pieces. Dust with flour, dip into the batter to coat and fry for 2–3 minutes until golden. Drain on kitchen paper, then dust with icing sugar and serve warm in a folded napkin, accompanied by the sauce.

Pear Charlotte

WATCHPOINTS
◆
Crème Pâtissière

SERVES 4

575 ml/1 pint water
125 g/4 oz caster sugar
$^1\!/_2$ lemon
3 small pears

Crème pâtissière:
450 ml/15 fl oz milk
$^1\!/_2$ vanilla pod, split open
5 egg yolks
75 g/3 oz caster sugar
75 g/3 oz plain flour

To line the mould:
10–12 thin slices white bread
50 g/2 oz soft butter
2 tbsp icing sugar

A delicious baked charlotte filled with crème pâtissière and diced pears.

———— ◆ ————

Measure the water into a saucepan, add the sugar and the juice of the lemon half and bring to the boil. Peel, halve and core the pears, and poach in the syrup for 15–20 minutes. Meanwhile, make the crème pâtissière (see page 27). Allow to cool.

When the pears are cooked, drain them, dice roughly and fold into the crème pâtissière. Set aside. Preheat the oven to 190°C/375°F/gas 5.

To prepare the mould, butter the bread, remove crusts, dust with icing sugar and toast evenly on both sides. From one slice, cut out a round to fit the bottom of a 1.1 litre/2 pint charlotte mould. Cut the remaining slices in half and stand upright, slightly overlapping, around the sides of the mould. Trim the pieces of bread so they will be level with the top of the mould. Fill with the crème pâtissière mixture.

Bake in the preheated oven for 50 minutes. Allow to cool slightly, then turn out on to a serving dish and serve warm.

French Custard Flan

WATCHPOINTS
◆
Crème Pâtissière ◆ Pastry

SERVES 6–8

1 recipe rich biscuit pastry
  (page 139)
2 recipes crème pâtissière (page 27)
icing sugar for sprinkling

The French have a passion for 'Flan'. Pronounced 'flohn' as in John, this simple confection consists of a thick slab of cold yellow crème pâtissière set on to a whisp of pastry.

———— ◆ ————

Preheat the oven to 200°C/400°F/gas 6. Roll out the pastry on a lightly floured work surface to a thickness of 6 mm/$^1\!/_4$ inch and use to line a deep 20 cm/8 inch flan tin (see page 140). Line the flan case with greaseproof paper, fill with baking beans and bake blind for 25–30 minutes.

Pour the hot crème pâtissière into the flan case and bake in the centre of the oven for 25–30 minutes or until the top of the filling is golden brown. Allow to cool, then cut into thick slices and sprinkle with icing sugar.

Pear Charlotte;
French Custard Flan.

'I have always maintained that there is nothing wrong with nursery food now that we are grown up and can have a glass of wine with it'

ELIZABETH RAY

The egg custard consists quite simply of eggs, milk and sugar, yet it is a most subtle, treasured confection, especially when it has been infused with the perfume of fresh vanilla.

The delicate flavour of egg custard has become a useful source of inspiration for the pastry cook, to create a number of unforgettable desserts. It can be baked into such dishes as crème caramel, bread and butter pudding and, of course, egg custard tart. The much admired crème brûlée has appeared on virtually everyone's menu since it became fashionable in the late seventies.

By enriching the basic mixture with egg yolks and cream, and flavouring the custard with coffee or chocolate, we arrive at the highly prized petits pots à la crème. Alternatively, the custard can be thickened over a gentle heat to make a fine smooth sauce.

Making a custard sauce is where many of us come unstuck. Yet it is worth trying again if things go wrong because this simple yet delicious preparation, if made correctly, forms the basis of some of our most delicate sauces, which in

3 Vanilla scented Egg Custard

to a dark rich rum and chocolate flummery

turn are incorporated into spectacular mousses, charlottes and puddings such as *Riz à l'impératrice* (page 41), flummeries and blancmanges.

Put aside, if you can, graven images of blancmange puddings as pallid and wobbly as the victimized faces to be seen lined up in school dining halls. The French have cared a little more for this preparation and, with due respect for the appetite, have chosen to refine it to a point of perfection. A blancmange need not stand up like a monument of white rubber; instead it should be enjoyed as a delicate mousse flavoured with fresh vanilla. Sample *Blanc-manger aux abricots* (page 41) and awful memories of school dinners will be erased.

Flummeries are one of the oldest desserts known. They started life as nothing more than a glorified gruel of milk, grain and honey. Today, however, we prefer our flummeries thickened with fine rice or semolina, enriched with egg yolks and cream and lightened with egg white.

The bavarois originated in Bavaria and became fashionable in Paris in the early part of the nineteenth century. To this day, it is known by pastry cooks the world over as the classic foundation from which the smoothest mousses and creams are made. The bavarois combines the subtle smoothness of egg custard with whipped cream, whisked egg whites and just enough gelatine to retain lightness. Although rather time-consuming to prepare, I can assure you that a bavarois is worth the effort.

The egg custard is also the foundation for the preparation of meltingly delicious ice creams, many of which can be made at home without the aid of expensive equipment.

One or two myths surround the making of egg custard, which I would like to dispel. Firstly, double boilers, *bain maries* and other fancy equipment are not needed for making egg custard. I am not saying that they do not work, rather that they are not necessary for a good result. Secondly, the temperature at which egg yolks cause milk to thicken is well below boiling point and any attempt to approach boiling will turn the custard into something akin to scrambled egg. Finally, the consistency of an egg custard should not be thicker than that of single cream.

Illustrated overleaf:
Riz a l'Impératrice;
Dark Rum and
Chocolate Flummery;
Blanc-manger aux
Apricots; Chocolate
Bavarois with
Vanilla-Poached
Pears.

1

Always measure all the ingredients carefully before commencing.

2

To prevent milk from catching, first rinse the saucepan out with cold water.

3

Any flavourings to be added are usually included with the milk.

4

To ensure even stirring, choose a flat wooden spoon that will fit neatly into the corners of the pan, where the custard is liable to catch.

5

Custards that are made without starch must never be allowed to come to the boil or they may curdle.

6

Always stir custard constantly while it is over heat.

7

The custard is cooked when it is just thick enough to coat the back of the spoon.

8

Saucepans carry residual heat which will spoil a custard if it is left to stand in the pan – even off the heat. When the correct consistency is reached, immediately transfer the custard to a clean bowl to arrest the thickening process.

9

Warm liquids take longer to cool in plastic containers than in metal or glass ones, so use a stainless steel or glass bowl to cool custard.

10

Never place a warm custard in the refrigerator to cool; it will raise the temperature, thus spoiling other foods and risking the development of harmful bacteria.

11

Instead let custard cool by placing the bowl in a basin of iced water.

12

Your first attempt at egg custard is never as good as your second. If at first you don't succeed, try again.

When learning a basic skill such as egg custard, be prepared to make mistakes. Provide yourself with plenty of eggs, milk and sugar and keep trying. Ingredients may be expensive at first, but when you do eventually get it right, your problems will be past and your money well spent.

Serve this delicate custard with poached fruit, sponge puddings, fruit tarts, etc.

MAKES 700 ml/1 1/2 pints
8 egg yolks
75 g/3 oz caster sugar
575 ml/1 pint milk
1/2 vanilla pod, split open, or
    3 drops of vanilla essence

1 Put the egg yolks into a 1 litre/1 3/4 pint bowl, ensuring that any clinging threads of egg white are removed. Add the sugar to

Egg Custard Sauce

the yolks and stir together until smooth. Bring the milk to the boil in a heavy saucepan, that has been rinsed out with water, with the vanilla pod or essence. When the milk has come to the boil, pour it steadily over the egg yolks and sugar, stirring continually with a flat wooden spoon.

2 Return the mixture to the saucepan and stir over a low heat for 45 seconds–1 minute, paying particular attention to the corners of the pan where the sauce is inclined to catch. The temperature at this stage is usually only a few degrees away from thickening. Make a note of the consistency of the custard as it falls from the spoon, and stir until the custard will only just coat the back of the spoon: it should be as thick as single cream. To test the consistency, run your index finger

across the coated spoon. When sufficiently thickened the finger mark will remain.

3 Without delay, strain the custard into a clean bowl to arrest the thickening process.

VARIATIONS

Caramel Custard Sauce: Omit the vanilla. Put 2 tbsp caster sugar into a heavy saucepan and place over a moderate heat to melt the sugar; stir until it begins to brown. Continue to add a further 4 tbsp sugar, a little at a time, stirring continually to dissolve, then allow to boil steadily to a dark caramel. Carefully stir into the boiling milk before adding it to the egg yolks. Reduce the sugar to 40 g/1¹/₂ oz. Serve cold with a compote of apples, pears, oranges or peaches.

Chocolate Custard Sauce: Omit the vanilla. Stir 125 g/4 oz of best quality plain chocolate into the boiling milk before adding it to the egg yolks. Reduce the sugar to 40 g/1¹/₂ oz. To enhance the flavour, stir 2 tbsp dark rum, whisky or cognac into the finished custard sauce. Serve hot with poached pears, poached soft meringues, steamed sponge puddings and banana fritters.

Coffee Custard Sauce: Omit the vanilla, and stir 2 tbsp instant coffee granules into the boiling milk before adding it to the egg yolks. To improve the flavour, add 2 tbsp Tia Maria or brandy to the finished custard. Serve warm with chocolate or coffee-flavoured sponge puddings, baked bananas or walnut tart.

Never leave a thickening custard sauce unattended – it should reach the correct consistency in less than 1 minute.

Blanc-manger aux Abricots

SERVES 6

225 ml/8 fl oz milk

25 g/1 oz white marzipan

1/2 vanilla pod, split open

3 eggs, at room temperature, separated

5 tbsp caster sugar

2 tsp powdered gelatine

2 tbsp cold water

2 tbsp Kirsch (optional)

400 g/14 oz canned apricot halves, drained

150 ml/5 fl oz double cream

This delicate French blanc-manger is a creamy white mousseline scented with almond, vanilla and Kirsch. It bears no relation to the uninspiring English blancmange — a jelly of cornflour and milk. Serve this subtly flavoured dessert in pretty stem glasses.

———— ◆ ————

Measure the milk into a heavy saucepan and add the marzipan and vanilla. Bring to a simmer, stirring until the marzipan has dissolved, 2–3 minutes. Mix the eggs yolks with 2 tbsp of the caster sugar. Pour the boiling milk over the egg mixture and stir evenly. Return to the saucepan and stir over a low heat until the custard will just coat the back of the spoon. Without delay strain the custard into a clean bowl.

Sprinkle the powdered gelatine over the cold water, allow to soften, then stir into the hot custard until dissolved. Stir in the Kirsch, if using, and allow to cool until beginning to set.

Reserve a few apricot halves for decoration. Roughly chop half of the rest and purée the remainder. Stir the chopped apricots into the purée and spoon into four pretty stem glasses.

To finish the blancmange, loosely whip the cream. Whisk the egg whites until they will hold their weight on the whisk, then add the remaining 3 tbsp sugar and continue whisking until soft peaks form. Stir the whipped cream into the setting custard and fold in the meringue.

Spoon the blanc-manger into 6 stem glasses and leave in the refrigerator to set for 1–1 1/2 hours. Slice the reserved apricot halves and use to decorate the mousses before serving.

Illustrated on page 37

VARIATION

During the summer when there is plenty of fresh fruit available, use fresh apricots or a mixture of peaches and raspberries.

Riz à l'Impératrice

SERVES 6

850 ml/1¹/₂ pints milk

15 g/¹/₂ oz marzipan (optional)

¹/₂ tsp vanilla essence

50 g/2 oz pudding rice, washed

50 g/2 oz chopped candied fruits,
  e.g. orange, lemon, pineapple,
  cherries, kiwi fruit

2 tbsp Kirsch

3 eggs, at room temperature,
  separated

125 g/4 oz caster sugar

1 tbsp powdered gelatine

2 tbsp cold water

150 ml/5 fl oz whipping cream

To decorate:

candied fruits

275 ml/¹/₂ pint set raspberry or
  redcurrant jelly (optional)

This is a classic dessert that is considered, by those who take their rice pudding seriously, to be a state-of-the-art masterpiece. Riz à l'Impératrice consists lusciously of a basic rice pudding cooked in milk, enriched with whipped cream and egg custard, lightened with whisked egg whites and held with gelatine. As if this isn't enough to worry the faint-hearted, pieces of candied fruits macerated in Kirsch are folded into the mixture.

———————— ◆ ————————

To prepare the rice pudding, measure 575 ml/1 pint of the milk into a heavy saucepan and bring to the boil. Add the marzipan, vanilla essence and rice. Stir back to the boil and simmer gently for 50 minutes until quite stiff, stirring occasionally. Allow to cool.

Macerate the chopped candied fruits in the Kirsch.

To prepare the custard, measure the remaining milk into a heavy saucepan and bring to the boil. Stir the egg yolks and 50 g/2 oz of the sugar together in a bowl and pour over the boiling milk. Return to the saucepan and stir over a low heat until the custard will just coat the back of the spoon. Without delay, pour the custard into a clean bowl.

Sprinkle the gelatine over the cold water and allow to soften, then stir into the hot custard until dissolved. Stir the custard over ice until it is beginning to set.

Whisk the egg whites until they will hold their weight on the whisk. Add the remaining sugar and continue whisking until soft peaks form. Fold the loosely whipped cream into the setting custard, then fold into the rice pudding. Finally fold in the meringue. Add the candied fruits and Kirsch. Turn into a 1.7 litre/3 pint jelly mould and refrigerate for 1¹/₂-2 hours until set.

To serve, dip the base of the mould into hot water for the count of 10 and turn out on to a serving dish. Arrange pieces of candied fruit, and chopped jelly if using, around the base to serve.

Illustrated on page 36

VARIATION

Chocolate Rice Bombe with Poached Pears: Proceed as above, melting 124 g/4 oz best quality plain chocolate in the hot custard and macerating the candied fruits in dark rum or brandy. When set, turn out and decorate with a border of poached pears, whipped cream and flaked chocolate.

Traditional Bread and Butter Pudding

SERVES 6

25 g/1 oz sultanas or raisins

1 sliced currant loaf, or 8 slices of
   white bread, crusts removed

50 g/2 oz soft butter

575 ml/1 pint milk

$\frac{1}{2}$ tsp vanilla essence

4 eggs

50 g/2 oz caster sugar

icing sugar for dusting

The maternal comforts of the egg custard are to be found beautifully set between soft layers of buttered bread in this much-loved pudding. Nursery puddings have become very popular in recent years, particularly with grown-ups who wish to relive a spoonful of their bygone days.

————— ◆ —————

Preheat the oven to 180°C/350°F/gas 4. Scatter the sultanas in a 900 ml/ 1$\frac{1}{2}$ pint pie dish. Butter bread generously and layer in the dish, overlapping the slices slightly.

   To make the custard, bring the milk to the boil with the vanilla essence in a heavy saucepan. Beat the eggs and sugar together in a bowl, pour in the milk and stir well. Strain the custard over the bread.

   Place the dish in a roasting pan and half fill the pan with boiling water. Bake in the preheated oven for 30–35 minutes or until the blade of a small knife inserted into the centre will come away cleanly. Dust with icing sugar and brown under a moderate grill. Serve warm.

Queen of Puddings

SERVES 4–6

150 g/5 oz fresh white or brown
   breadcrumbs

25 g/1 oz butter, cut into small
   pieces

575 ml/1 pint milk

$\frac{1}{2}$ tsp vanilla essence

5 eggs, at room temperature

125 g/4 oz caster sugar

4 tbsp raspberry jam

This most glamorous of puddings is so-named because its topping of meringue, jewelled with jam and toasted until golden, was thought fit for a queen.

————— ◆ —————

Preheat the oven to 180°C/350°F/gas 4. Scatter the breadcrumbs over the bottom of a 900 ml/1$\frac{1}{2}$ pint pie dish and sprinkle pieces of butter over the top.

   Bring the milk to the boil with vanilla essence in a heavy saucepan. Separate three of the eggs and add the remaining two whole eggs to the yolks with half of the sugar. Beat lightly together. Pour the boiling milk over the egg mixture and stir until evenly mixed. Strain the custard over the buttered breadcrumbs in the pie dish.

Queen of Puddings; Traditional Bread and Butter Pudding.

Place the dish in a roasting pan and half fill the pan with boiling water. Bake in the preheated oven for 30–35 minutes.

To finish, whisk the three egg whites until they will hold their weight on the whisk. Gradually add the remaining sugar and continue whisking until the meringue will form stiff peaks. Spoon the meringue into a piping bag fitted with a 1 cm/¹/₂ inch nozzle and pipe parallel lines over the top of the pudding.

Spoon the raspberry jam into the spaces between the meringue and place the dish under a preheated moderate grill until the meringue is golden. Serve warm.

Dark Rum and Chocolate Flummery

WATCHPOINTS
◆
Egg Custard ◆ Meringue

SERVES 6

3 eggs, at room temperature,
    separated
60 g/2^1/$_2$ oz caster sugar
575 ml/1 pint milk
3 tbsp ground rice or semolina
3 tbsp dark rum
175 g/6 oz best quality plain
    chocolate, broken into pieces
150 ml/5 fl oz double cream, lightly
    whipped

To decorate:
50 g/2 oz best quality plain
    chocolate, flaked
icing sugar for dusting

Flavoured with dark rum and chocolate, this delicious flummery will soon find its way to the gourmet's table where it belongs.

―――――◆―――――

Put the egg yolks into a bowl and stir in 2 tbsp of the caster sugar. Bring the milk to the boil in a heavy saucepan. Sprinkle over the ground rice or semolina and stir for 5 minutes to thicken. Stir into the egg yolks and sugar. Add the rum and chocolate and stir until melted. Allow to cool.

Whisk the egg whites until they will hold their weight on the whisk, then whisk in the remaining 3 tbsp sugar a little at a time, until soft peaks form. Fold the whipped cream into the cool flummery followed by the meringue.

Turn the flummery into a serving bowl and chill for 1 hour to set. Decorate with flaked chocolate and dust with sifted icing sugar before serving.

Illustrated on page 36

French Toast
in bed with Cherries and Custard

WATCHPOINTS
◆
Egg Custard

SERVES 6

1 small white loaf, crusts removed
50 g/2 oz butter, softened
400 g/14 oz bottled cherries, drained
    and stoned

Custard:
575 ml/1 pint milk
3 drops vanilla essence
4 eggs
50 g/2 oz caster sugar

To finish:
1 tsp ground cinnamon
2 tbsp caster sugar

I cannot think of a better place to discover cherries than in a smooth egg custard, surrounded by soft layers of French toast.

―――――◆―――――

Preheat the oven to 180°C/350°F/gas 4. Cut the loaf into 2 cm/^{3}/$_4$ inch thick slices and butter well.

Arrange the slices in a 25.5 cm/10 inch round pie dish, overlapping them in a ring to leave a well in the centre. Place the cherries in the well.

To make the custard, bring the milk to the boil with the vanilla essence in a heavy saucepan. Beat the eggs and sugar together in a bowl. Pour the boiling milk over the eggs and stir well. Strain, then pour the custard over the bread and cherries.

Stand the pie dish in a roasting pan and half fill the pan with boiling water. Bake in the preheated oven for 35–40 minutes or until a knife inserted into the middle will come away cleanly.

Combine the ground cinnamon with the caster sugar and sprinkle over the top. Serve warm.

Chocolate Bavarois with Vanilla-Poached Pears

WATCHPOINTS

◆

Egg Custard ◆ Meringue

A bavarois takes time to prepare, but is a sumptuous dessert. I have set this one in a charlotte mould with plain chocolate, a dice of poached pears and a handful of brandy-soaked macaroons.

——————— ◆ ———————

To poach the pears, put the water in a saucepan with the sugar, vanilla and lemon juice or vitamin C tablet. Bring to the boil. Peel the pears, halve and remove the core and stem with a melon-baller. Add to the syrup, cover with a circle of greaseproof paper and poach for 15–20 minutes. When tender, leave to cool in the syrup.

To prepare the bavarois, mix the egg yolks with 50 g/2 oz sugar in a bowl. Bring the milk to the boil in a heavy saucepan. Pour over the egg yolk and sugar mixture, stirring well. Return to the saucepan and stir over a low heat until the custard will just coat the back of the spoon. Pour into a glass bowl, add the chocolate and stir until melted.

Soften the gelatine in the cold water, then stir into the chocolate custard until dissolved. Stir the custard over ice until it is beginning to set.

Remove two pear halves from the syrup and dice evenly. Whisk the egg whites until they will hold their weight on the whisk. Add the remaining sugar and continue whisking until soft peaks form. Fold the loosely whipped cream into the setting custard, followed by the meringue. Add the diced pears and the brandy-soaked macaroons. Turn into a 1.1 litre/2 pint charlotte mould or pudding basin, cover and chill for 1½–2 hours until set.

To finish the bavarois, dip the base of the mould into hot water for the count of 10 and turn out on to a serving dish. Drain and slice the remaining pears. Whip the whipping cream with the caster sugar and spread on top of the bavarois. Decorate with pear slices. Sprinkle the sides with flaked chocolate. Serve accompanied by the remaining pears.

Illustrated on page 37

SERVES 8

575 ml/1 pint water

125 g/4 oz caster sugar

½ vanilla pod, or 1 tsp vanilla essence

juice of ½ lemon or ½ 50 mg vitamin C tablet

4 Comice pears

Chocolate bavarois:

4 eggs, at room temperature, separated

125 g/4 oz caster sugar

350 ml/12 fl oz milk

150 g/5 oz best quality plain chocolate, in pieces

1 tbsp powdered gelatine

2 tbsp cold water

150 ml/5 fl oz double cream, loosely whipped

4 small macaroons, soaked in 2 tbsp brandy, eau-de-vie de Poire or Amaretto

To decorate:

150 ml/5 fl oz whipping cream

1 tbsp caster sugar

200 g/7 oz plain chocolate, flaked

Crème Brûlée aux Fruits des Bois

WATCHPOINTS
—— ◆ ——
Egg Custard

SERVES 4
175 g/6 oz raspberries, blueberries or
    alpine strawberries
6 egg yolks
2 tbsp caster sugar
275 ml/10 fl oz double cream
1/2 vanilla pod, split
125 g/4 oz demerara sugar

To decorate:
berry fruits

My favourite crème brûlée is as smooth and as near liquid yellow as an over-ripe Normandy cheese and contains a wave of soft berry fruits. The best caramel tops are crisp and dark with a slight bitter taste.

——————— ◆ ———————

Divide the fruit between four 9 cm/3 1/2 inch diameter ramekins.

Place the egg yolks in a bowl and stir in the sugar with a hand whisk. Put the cream and vanilla pod in a heavy saucepan and bring to the boil. Pour over the egg yolks and stir until evenly mixed.

Pour the custard back into the saucepan and stir over a low heat until it will just coat the back of the spoon, 20–30 seconds. Without delay, strain into the flameproof dishes and chill to set.

Sprinkle the demerara sugar evenly over the custards and place under a hot grill to caramelize. Chill before serving, decorated with berry fruits.

Petits Pots de Crème au Chocolat; Crème Brûlée aux Fruits des Bois.

Petits Pots de Crème au Chocolat

WATCHPOINTS
—— ◆ ——
Egg Custard

MAKES 8
575 ml/1 pint milk
4 egg yolks
1 egg
50 g/2 oz caster sugar
3 tbsp cold water
125 g/4 oz best quality plain
    chocolate, broken into pieces

To decorate:
whipped cream
chopped nuts
chocolate leaves (optional)

Preheat the oven to 180°C/350°F/gas 4. Arrange eight custard pots or ramekin dishes in a roasting pan and set side.

Bring the milk to the boil in a heavy saucepan. Mix three of the egg yolks, the whole egg and 25 g/1 oz of the sugar in a bowl. Pour over the boiling milk, stirring evenly.

Dissolve the remaining sugar in the water over low heat. Remove from the heat and stir in the chocolate until melted, followed by the remaining egg yolk. Stir a little of the custard into the chocolate mixture, then combine with the remainder.

Strain the custard into a jug and pour into the custard pots or ramekins. Half fill the roasting pan with boiling water and place in the preheated oven for 25–30 minutes or until the custards seem firm when the sides of the pots are tapped. Allow to cool and chill before serving. Decorate with piped cream rosettes, chopped nuts and chocolate leaves if desired.

Bring me an egg custard and a freezer and I will show you how to make the smoothest, most delicious ice cream that ever melted in your mouth. Home-made ice creams are quite different from commercially produced so-called 'dairy' ice creams, which are as far removed from cream and the dairy as they are riddled with artificial flavourings, preservatives and stabilizers.

It is a sad fact in this age of modern living that many of our favourite foods are not what they once were. Ice cream as it used to be has almost disappeared, to be replaced by 'soft whip', 'soft scoop', and even low-fat polyunsaturated ice cream for slimmers. Whatever next? The only way to combat this plague of deception is to put into the mouths of the deceived a taste of *real* dairy ice cream – made with milk, cream, egg yolks and sugar. A new generation of children will then grow up with a liking for foods that taste of what they are and not a string of E numbers.

The principle of making ice cream is the same as for sorbet: a solution containing a specific amount of sugar is frozen against the inside of a metal bowl. It is important that the amount of sugar is correct since it is the sugar density that determines the freezing capacity of the solution. Too much sugar and the solution will not freeze. Insufficient sugar and it will freeze solidly like ice. As the solution, in this case a fine egg custard, freezes into tiny crystals against the metal bowl, they are stirred back into the unfrozen custard until it thickens gradually into a smooth cream.

If you are hooked on homemade ice cream as I am, you will want to own a domestic ice cream machine. They are expensive but are worth their weight in gold for the deliciously smooth ice cream they produce.

As you become better acquainted with the art of ice-cream-making,

Perfect, smooth

Ice Cream

you will be tempted to experiment by adding different flavours to the egg custard. Chocolate, caramel, strawberry and raspberry are particularly good, while toasted almond, hazelnut and walnut brittle border on the sublime and join the likes of black cherry and Kirsch, and soft prune and Armagnac. When you exhaust these variations, you can move on to discover the unlimited possibilities of the sorbet . . .

The success of the sorbet, and in recent years the yogurt ice, is due to our need to be refreshed at the end of a meal, when the palate cries out for something sweet yet sharp, cold and fruity. In his *Guide to Modern Cookery*, Georges Auguste Escoffier maintained that sorbets, 'when well prepared and daintily dished, are the consummation of all that is delicate and good'.

Homemade sorbets and ices are not, as many people suppose, difficult to make without an expensive ice-cream-making machine. They are, in fact, quite successfully achieved with just a whisk, a metal bowl and a freezer. It is true that ices and sorbets made by hand are never as smooth and fine as those made in a machine, but they are still well worth the effort.

The first sorbets and water ices were made by the Italians in the sixteenth century. These early ices were simply flavoured syrups frozen over crushed ice and salt. The result was not dissimilar to our modern-day granita, which consists of a semi-frozen syrup stirred into a granular slush. Granitas may be flavoured with any number of fresh fruit purées, syrups and dessert wines.

Yogurt ices are becoming more and more popular, with the increased emphasis on healthy eating, and they are easier to make than ice creams and sorbets. I admit that I am not very keen on yogurt on its own, but when it is frozen together with fruit and sugar, I can eat it until the cows come home.

Illustrated overleaf:
Prune and Armagnac
Bombe with a
Toasted Walnut
Centre; Ice Cream
Meringue Layer Cake;
Raspberry Sorbet;
Vanilla Ice Cream in
a decorative ice bowl.

refreshing, tangy
& Sorbet

1

If you are investing in an electric ice cream maker, spend as much as you can afford.

2

A light sugar syrup freezes into a hard ice; a syrup containing too much sugar does not freeze at all. Therefore, it is important to use the correct amount of sugar so that an ice cream or sorbet will freeze into a soft consistency.

3

Alcohol does not freeze, so do not be tempted to add more than is stated in a recipe.

4

When using acid fruits, avoid contact with bare metals other than stainless steel and those coated with enamel.

5

Stainless steel and enamel bowls are good conductors of heat and cold, and therefore hasten the freezing of ices and sorbets. Plastic and glass bowls have the opposite effect.

6

If using an electric ice cream maker, allow 25–40 minutes to freeze 1 litre/ 1^3/$_4$ pints ice cream, depending on the model.

7

Ices should be stored in covered plastic containers in the ice-making compartment of the refrigerator. If stored in the deep freeze, they will harden beyond use.

8

If ices and sorbets become too hard to serve, leave them at room temperature for 20–30 minutes before serving.

9

Homemade ices and sorbets are best eaten on the day they are made, or soon after, as they have a tendency to harden if kept for any length of time.

10

If you need to transport ice cream or sorbet any distance, wrap the container first in wet newspaper and pack with plenty of ice.

The dark brown vanilla pod has a very special aroma and is used to impart a strong syrupy flavour to custards, creams and fine biscuits. The true flavour of the vanilla pod is released by splitting the pod from top to bottom and scraping out a thick paste of what amounts to thousands of tiny black seeds. It is these harmless seeds that provide the pretty speckled appearance and excellent flavour in the finest vanilla ice cream.

MAKES 1 litre/1^3/$_4$ pints
425 ml/15 fl oz milk
275 ml/10 fl oz double cream
^{1}/$_2$ vanilla pod
150 g/5 oz caster sugar
8 egg yolks

1 Measure the milk and cream into a heavy saucepan that has first been rinsed out with cold water. Bring to the boil.

If the vanilla pod is dry and will not split easily, allow it to soften first in the milk for 5–10 minutes. Split the pod with a small knife and scrape out the black seeds on to a chopping board. With the side of the knife, rub the seeds into 1 tsp of the caster sugar until the seeds are evenly dispersed. Place the vanilla sugar together with the remaining

Vanilla Ice Cream

sugar and the egg yolks in a bowl and stir together until smooth.

2 When the milk and cream mixture has come to the boil, pour it over the egg yolks and sugar and stir until evenly mixed. Return the custard to the saucepan and stir over a low heat with a flat wooden

spoon until the custard will just coat the back of the spoon. Thickening should not take longer than 1 minute. Without delay, strain the custard into a clean bowl to arrest the thickening process. Allow the custard to cool completely.

3 Pour the custard into a stainless steel or enamel bowl and freeze for 45 minutes. Stir the custard with a hand whisk to loosen any that is beginning to freeze against the bowl.

Return to the freezer and freeze for a further 1 hour 40 minutes, stirring every 20 minutes until firm.

4 Transfer the ice cream to a plastic container and store in the ice compartment of the refrigerator (not the freezer) until ready to serve.

VARIATIONS

Chocolate Ice Cream: Melt 125 g/4 oz best quality plain chocolate in the custard. Cool and freeze as above.

Caramel Ice Cream: Omit the vanilla and 50 g/2 oz sugar. Stir 4 tbsp of caramel (see page 69) into the custard. Cool and freeze as above.

Almond or Hazelnut Brittle Ice Cream: As the ice cream begins to firm in the freezer, stir in 75 g/3 oz crushed almond or hazelnut brittle (see page 69). Freeze until firm.

Black Cherry and Kirsch Ice Cream: Omit the vanilla. Allow the custard to cool, then stir in 150 g/5 oz roughly chopped stoned black cherries and 2 tbsp of Kirsch. Freeze as above.

Prune and Armagnac Ice Cream: Soak 175 g/6 oz cooked prunes in 50 ml/2 fl oz Armagnac for at least 24 hours, then chop roughly, discarding the stones. Omit the vanilla from the basic recipe, add the prunes and Armagnac to the cooled custard and freeze as above.

Strawberry or Raspberry Ice Cream: Omit the vanilla. Allow the custard to cool, then stir in 225 g/8 oz crushed strawberries or raspberries. Freeze as above.

Strawberry Yogurt Ice

SERVES 6–8

275 g/10 oz strawberries,
   fresh or frozen
50 g/2 oz icing sugar, sifted
275 ml/10 fl oz plain yogurt
finely grated zest and juice
   of ½ orange

Hull the strawberries and cut them in half. Purée the berries together with the icing sugar in a food processor or blender. Add the yogurt and orange zest and juice and blend until smooth.

For best results, freeze the mixture in an electric ice cream maker, allowing about 25 minutes until firm. If you do not have an ice cream maker, transfer the mixture to a stainless steel or enamel bowl and freeze for 1 hour or until the mixture begins to freeze around the edges.

Whisk well to break down the ice crystals evenly. Return to the freezer and freeze for a further 1–1½ hours, whisking every 20 minutes, until firm.

Transfer the yogurt ice to a plastic container, cover and store in the ice compartment of your refrigerator.

VARIATION

Raspberry Yogurt Ice: Replace strawberries with raspberries. Omit the orange. After puréeing the raspberries with the icing sugar, sieve to remove pips. Freeze as above.

Blackcurrant Yogurt Ice

SERVES 4–6

175 g/6 oz blackcurrants, fresh,
   frozen or canned
75 ml/3 fl oz water
75 g/3 oz granulated sugar
275 ml/10 fl oz plain yogurt

If using fresh or frozen blackcurrants, place them in a stainless steel saucepan with the water and sugar, cover and simmer for 6–8 minutes. Rub the soft berries through a nylon sieve together with their juices. If using canned blackcurrants, just sieve them with their syrup. Combine the blackcurrant purée with the yogurt.

For best results, freeze in an electric ice cream maker. If you do not have an ice cream maker, transfer the mixture to a stainless steel or enamel bowl and freeze for 1 hour or until the mixture begins to freeze around the edges. Whisk well to break down the ice crystals evenly. Return to the freezer and freeze for a further 1-1½ hours, whisking every 20 minutes, until firm.

Transfer the yogurt ice to a plastic container, cover and store in the ice compartment of your refrigerator until ready to use.

Strawberry Yogurt Ice;
Blackcurrant Yogurt Ice.

Blackcurrant and Pear Sorbet

SERVES 6
200 g/7 oz canned blackcurrants in
   syrup
400 g/14 oz canned pears in syrup
125 g/4 oz caster sugar

A cool, refreshing dessert for long summer evenings. Serve in tall stemmed glasses with a splash of Crème de Cassis.

———————— ◆ ————————

Drain the syrup from the blackcurrants and the pears into a stainless steel or enamel saucepan, add the sugar and simmer, stirring, until dissolved. Place the blackcurrants and pears in a food processor or blender and purée until smooth. Combine the purée with the syrup and allow to cool.

For best results, freeze in an electric ice cream maker. If you do not have an ice cream maker, transfer the mixture to a stainless steel or enamel bowl and freeze for 1 hour or until the mixture is just beginning to freeze at the edges. Whisk well to break down the ice crystals evenly. Return to the freezer and freeze for a further $1^1/_2$–2 hours, whisking every 30 minutes, until firm.

Transfer the sorbet to a plastic container, cover and store in the ice compartment of your refrigerator.

Raspberry Sorbet

SERVES 6
900 g/2 lb raspberries, fresh or frozen
125 g/4 oz caster sugar

Unlike many sorbet recipes that you may come across, this one is made from pure fruit and is not diluted with water. The flavour is, of course, much stronger and all the more delicious.

The deep colour of raspberries improves considerably when they are simmered with sugar. Simmering does not appear to affect their flavour.

———————— ◆ ————————

Put the raspberries together with the sugar into a stainless steel or enamel saucepan. Stir over a low heat until the juices begin to run and continue to simmer for 2–3 minutes. Remove from the heat and let cool slightly.

Purée the fruit in a blender or food processor, then rub through a fine nylon sieve to remove the pips. Allow the purée to cool.

For best results, freeze in an electric ice cream maker. If you do not have an ice cream maker, transfer the mixture to a stainless steel or enamel bowl and freeze for 1 hour or until the mixture is beginning to freeze around the edges. Whisk well to break down the ice crystals evenly. Return to the freezer for a further $1^1/_2$–2 hours, whisking every 30 minutes, until firm.

Transfer the sorbet to a plastic container, cover and store in the ice compartment of your refrigerator until ready to use. Scoop into chilled glass dishes to serve. Brandy snaps (page 156) go well with this sorbet.

Illustrated on page 50

Strawberry Sorbet

WATCHPOINTS
◆
Ice Cream & Sorbet

SERVES 6
900 g/2 lb strawberries, fresh or
    frozen
125 g/4 oz icing sugar, sifted
juice of 1 lemon
2 tbsp Grand Marnier (optional)

Strawberry sorbet is particularly tasty served with fresh pineapple moistened with Kirsch or Grand Marnier. Crisp dessert biscuits, such as almond tuiles (page 155), make an ideal accompaniment.

◆

Hull the strawberries, halve them and purée in a food processor or blender with the icing sugar and lemon juice. Add the Grand Marnier if using.

For best results, freeze in an electric ice cream maker. If you do not have an ice cream maker, transfer mixture to a stainless steel or enamel bowl and freeze for 1 hour or until the mixture is beginning to freeze at the edges.

Whisk well to break down the ice crystals evenly. Return to the freezer and freeze for a further $1^1/_2$–2 hours, whisking every 30 minutes, until firm.

Transfer the sorbet to a plastic container, cover and store in the ice compartment of your refrigerator until required.

SERVING SUGGESTION

A decorative ice bowl makes an impressive serving dish for ices and sorbets (as shown on pages 6 and 51). To make one you will need 3 freezerproof bowls, fractionally different in size. Pour water into the largest one to a depth of 1 cm/$^1/_2$ inch and freeze until firm. Position medium bowl in larger one, fill gap with water, weight down and freeze until firm. Pour warm water into inside bowl to loosen, then remove. Press flowers, herbs, citrus fruit slices, etc, onto ice. Position small bowl in ice bowl, fill gap with water, weight down and freeze until firm. Remove small bowl and fill ice bowl with sorbet or ice cream to serve.

Lemon Sorbet

SERVES 4–6
575 ml/1 pint water
225 g/8 oz granulated sugar
275 ml/10 fl oz fresh lemon juice
(5–6 large lemons)

*Orange Sorbet in ice bowl;
Lemon Sorbet;
Lime Sorbet;
Pineapple Sorbet Wedges.*

Measure the water and sugar into a saucepan and bring to a simmer, stirring until dissolved. Allow the syrup to cool completely, then stir in the lemon juice and strain.

Transfer the mixture to a stainless steel or enamel bowl and freeze for 1 hour or until the mixture is just beginning to set at the edges. Whisk well to break down the ice crystals evenly. Return to the freezer and freeze for a further $1\frac{1}{2}$–2 hours, whisking every 30 minutes, until firm.

Transfer the sorbet to a plastic container, cover and store in the ice compartment of your refrigerator until required.

VARIATIONS:
Orange Sorbet: Replace the lemon juice with freshly squeezed orange Juice.
Lime Sorbet: Replace the lemon juice with freshly squeezed lime juice and 1–2 drops green food colouring.

Pineapple Sorbet Wedges

SERVES 6
150 ml/5 fl oz water
75 g/3 oz granulated sugar
1 large pineapple
2 tbsp Kirsch

Measure the water and sugar into a saucepan, bring to the boil, stirring to dissolve the sugar, and simmer for 2–3 minutes. Pour the syrup into a metal bowl and cool over ice. In the meantime, cut the pineapple in half lengthwise, discard core and spoon out flesh. Set the pineapple skins aside. Place the flesh in a blender or food processor and work until smooth. Transfer to a measuring jug and top up if necessary with water to make 250 ml/9 fl oz.

Stir the pineapple juice and Kirsch into the cool syrup and freeze for 30 minutes or until the mixture is beginning to set at the edges.

Remove sorbet from freezer and whisk to break up any pieces of ice. Return to the freezer and freeze for a further $1\frac{1}{2}$ hours, whisking every 30 minutes, until slushy. Pile the sorbet into the pineapple shells, spread level and freeze for 1 hour or until firm.

To serve, cut each pineapple half into 3 wedges and keep in the ice compartment of the refrigerator until needed.

Blackcurrant Granita

SERVES 6
125 g/4 oz fresh blackcurrants
225 g/8 oz caster sugar
1 litre/1³/₄ pints water
75 ml/3 fl oz blackcurrant syrup

Granitas are wonderfully refreshing water ices with a granular texture. Although easy to make, granitas are inclined to set solidly if stored for any length of time. To enjoy them at their best, eat soon after making.

———————— ♦ ————————

Put the blackcurrants, sugar and water into a saucepan, bring to the boil, stirring to dissolve the sugar; simmer for 3–4 minutes. Stir in the blackcurrant syrup. Strain into a metal bowl and cool.

Pour the cold syrup into a stainless steel tray and put in the coldest part of your freezer. The syrup will begin to freeze after about 1 hour; at this stage, stir the semi-frozen ice crystals well with a metal spoon. Return to the freezer and stir every 30 minutes until the crystals form an even mass and the granita will hold together. Store the granita in the least cold part of your freezer until ready to serve.

To serve, give the granita a final stir to break up any large pieces of ice. Divide between dessert glasses and serve with langues de chat (page 156).

Blackcurrant Granita;
Gerwürztraminer Granita.

Gerwürztraminer Granita

SERVES 6
175 g/6 oz caster sugar
50 ml/2 fl oz water
finely grated zest and juice
    of ¹/₂ orange
finely grated zest and juice
    of ¹/₂ lemon
1 bottle (750 ml) Gerwürztraminer

Gerwürztraminer is a distinctive wine from Alsace that has a spicy, often flowery bouquet. To capture its lively character freeze this wine into a simple granita. For a special dinner party, try serving it between courses to refresh the palate.

———————— ♦ ————————

Put the sugar and water into a saucepan and add the citrus zest and juice. Bring to the boil, stirring to dissolve the sugar, and simmer for 3–4 minutes. Let cool in a metal bowl.

Add the Gerwürztraminer and strain into a stainless steel tray. Freeze and store as for blackcurrant granita (above).

To serve, give the granita a final stir to break up any large pieces of ice, then spoon into stemmed dessert glasses.

Prune and Armagnac Bombe
with a Toasted Walnut Centre

SERVES 6

¹/₂ recipe vanilla ice cream (page 53)

¹/₂ recipe prune and Armagnac ice
cream (page 53)

125 g/4 oz walnut halves

2 tbsp maple or golden syrup

To decorate:

10–12 walnut halves

10–12 prunes, soaked in Armagnac

Ice cream bombes are perfect for special occasions, when they are brought to the table with a great deal of pomp and ceremony as everyone waits to see what is inside. Frozen desserts do, of course, take time to prepare, but they have the advantage that they can be prepared well ahead of time. Fillings can be varied according to taste, although it is important to choose attractive colours with complementary flavours.

———————— ◆ ————————

Chill a 1.1 litre/2 pint bombe mould in the freezer.

Soften the vanilla ice cream to a spreading consistency. Fill a large bowl with ice and stand the bombe mould in the centre to keep it cold. Smooth the vanilla ice cream against the inside of the mould in an even layer all over, using a tablespoon. Return to the freezer to firm for 15–20 minutes.

Soften the prune and Armagnac ice cream to a spreading consistency. Replace the bombe mould in the bowl of ice, and spread the prune ice cream over the vanilla to form an even layer. Leave a well in the centre. Return to the freezer until firm.

To prepare the walnut centre, roughly chop the walnuts. Spread out the nuts on a baking sheet and toast them under a hot grill to release their flavour. Allow to cool, then combine with the maple or golden syrup to form a thick paste. Spoon the paste into the centre of the bombe and return to the freezer.

To serve the bombe, dip the mould in hot water for the count of 10, and turn out on to a serving plate. Decorate the top and base of the bombe with walnut halves and prunes soaked in Armagnac.

Illustrated on page 50

Old-fashioned bombe moulds can be found in antique shops. They come in various shapes and sizes — the best ones are made from tin-lined copper

Ice Cream Meringue Layer Cake

WATCHPOINTS

◆

Ice Cream & Sorbet ◆ Meringue

SERVES 6–8

4 egg whites, at room temperature

225 g/8 oz caster sugar

500 ml/18 fl oz (¹/₂ recipe) vanilla ice cream (page 53)

500 ml/18 fl oz (¹/₂ recipe) chocolate ice cream (page 53)

500 ml/18 fl oz (¹/₂ recipe) strawberry ice cream (page 53)

To finish:

275 ml/10 fl oz double cream

1 tbsp caster sugar

50 g/2 oz flaked almonds, toasted strawberry slices or candied fruits

One of the most surprising features of meringue is its ability to freeze and still remain crisp. The Italians were amongst the first to make use of this new-found sensation and have incorporated it into their much-acclaimed Torta di Gelato, or Ice Cream Meringue Layer Cake, known for its multitude of flavours and textures.

◆

Preheat the oven to 140°C/275°F/gas 1. Line two wooden baking trays with non-stick baking parchment, or line 2 metal trays with 3–4 sheets of newspaper and then with parchment. Draw four 20 cm/8 inch circles on the paper, using a plate as a guide, and put on one side.

Whisk the egg whites in a clean mixing bowl until they will hold their weight on the whisk. Add the sugar a little at a time and continue whisking until stiff. Spread or pipe the meringue inside the marked circles on the paper. Dry in the preheated oven for 15 minutes, then reduce the temperature to 120°C/250°F/gas ¹/₂ and dry for a further 2–3 hours. Allow to cool completely.

To assemble the cake, turn the vanilla ice cream out of its container on to a sheet of greaseproof paper and cut into thick slices. Cover one meringue layer with the ice cream slices and position another meringue circle on top. Cover it with slices of chocolate ice cream. Top with the third meringue circle and then with slices of strawberry ice cream. Cover with the final meringue circle. Freeze until the ice cream is firm.

Loosely whip the cream with the sugar and use to cover the top and sides of the cake, saving enough to pipe on top. Cover the sides with toasted flaked almonds. Decorate the top with piped cream and strawberry slices, or candied fruits.

Return to the freezer until ready to serve. It may be necessary to allow the cake to soften at room temperature for 15–20 minutes. To test for softness, insert a wooden skewer into the centre.

Illustrated on page 50

VARIATION

Sandwich hazelnut brittle ice cream (page 53) between layers of chocolate meringue, cover with cream and decorate with flaked chocolate.

'There is no love sincerer than the love of food'

GEORGE BERNARD SHAW

Caramel is that moment of perfection that occurs before sugar burns. A form of caramel can be produced from all ingredients that contain natural sugars. Flour, for instance, contains a sugar called maltose, which will brown readily given sufficient heat. This explains the golden appearance of a loaf of bread as it comes out of the oven. Cakes, biscuits and pastries, most of which contain sugar, are subject to caramelization as they are baking. In fact, it is caramel that accounts for most of the delicious aromas that we savour in a busy kitchen.

Caramel is indispensable for the preparation of so many delicious desserts and pastries. Too often our desire for caramel is limited to the occasional visit to a French pâtisserie or restaurant where this gorgeous mahogany brown substance finds its way layered into baked egg custards, spooned over fluffy white meringues or incorporated into wonderful cream sauces.

Nearly everyone, it seems, has a passion for caramel in one form or another, but relatively few cooks have found out how to make it for themselves. The ingredients couldn't be more simple, so why is caramel not prepared more often in the home? The experienced cook will tell you that caramel is easy, and I suppose it is, providing you have been shown how to make it properly. The reason why caramel does not appear very often in less specialized recipe books is that, without proper instruction and guidance, caramel is considered to be rather dangerous to prepare. Indeed it is, if not handled with due

Smooth, crème
Caramel

care. In this section I have set out in detail a series of watchpoints and safety precautions essential for the preparation of successful caramel.

To make pure caramel, refined sugars are used and the process of browning the sugar is controlled in a saucepan to produce a mahogany brown liquid. When the caramel is cooled it will set hard.

If a simple caramel sauce is required, a quantity of water is stirred in to prevent it setting into a brittle. Caramel sauce is an indispensable preparation and is most useful for creating off-the-cuff desserts. I most often use it to flavour mousses, creams and custards, as well as to pour over ice cream. It keeps particularly well, so I often keep a quantity of caramel sauce on hand in a glass jar or bottle.

If, instead of adding water, a measured quantity of butter and cream is stirred into the boiling caramel, the mixture becomes butterscotch. This is equally delicious used to flavour custards, mousses and creams, or used as a topping for sponge puddings or ice creams. I have come across a surprising number of butterscotch recipes that do little to remind me of the true flavour of butterscotch. For real butterscotch sauce there should only be three ingredients – sugar, butter and cream – and possibly one or two sticky fingers.

Nut brittles – croquant or praline as they are known in French pâtisserie – are made by stirring toasted nuts into liquid caramel. The mixture is then poured on to an oiled baking sheet and allowed to set hard. Nut brittles keep very well in an airtight jar. Apart from being delicious confections in their own right, pralines can be crushed and sprinkled over ice creams, or used to flavour a variety of mousses, creams and fillings.

Illustrated overleaf: Walnut Sponge Pudding with Butterscotch; Creme Caramel; Almond and Hazelnut Brittles; Chocolate Mousse with Hazelnut Praline.

& Praline
addictive

1

Boiling sugar is extremely hot, so please be careful. In particular, keep children out of the kitchen when making caramel.

2

Read through the recipe and have everything ready before you start.

3

Choose a large heavy saucepan preferably of stainless steel or copper. Aluminium is not suitable.

4

To ensure the saucepan is free from grease, rub the inside with a cut lemon and a spoonful of salt. Rinse with cold water.

5

Open packets of sugar often contain traces of flour and other debris which may cause the caramel to crystallize, so open a fresh packet if possible.

6

Avoid getting any caramel up the sides of the saucepan; it is likely to burn and produce a lot of unpleasant smoke.

7

Never leave caramel unattended on the stove.

8

To prevent splashing, use a long-handled wooden spoon and cover your hand with a folded tea towel.

9

To clean a saucepan that has been used for caramel fill with water and let simmer on the stove for 10–15 minutes.

IN THE EVENT OF AN ACCIDENT

If the caramel starts to burn and smoke furiously, immediately cover your hand with a folded tea towel and remove the caramel from the heat.

◆

Calmly pour the caramel into a waste bin containing vegetable or other debris. Alternatively, take the pan outside and pour the caramel over an area of damp soil. Open windows and doors to disperse smoke.

◆

Do not pour the caramel down the sink and never try to cool the caramel down with water – the resulting clouds of steam may burn you.

This master recipe forms the basis for all of the recipes in this section and is also referred to in other sections where caramel and nut brittle or praline are called for.

MAKES 75 ml/3 fl oz
150 g/5 oz caster sugar

1 First, fill a large bowl or sink with cold water ready to cool the caramel.

2 Measure 2 tbsp of the sugar into a heavy stainless steel, copper or enamel saucepan. Place over a moderate heat to melt the sugar and stir until it begins to brown. Continue to add the sugar a little at a time, stirring continually to

dissolve. When all the sugar has been added, allow the caramel to boil steadily to an even golden, mahogany brown.

3 Without delay, immerse the base of the saucepan in the sink or bowl filled with cold water until boiling has stopped. This may take 2–3 minutes. At this stage the caramel will begin to set and may be used for dipping or for the preparation of nut brittles. If the caramel becomes too firm, reheat gently on the stove to melt.

VARIATIONS
Almond Brittle or Praline: Lightly oil a baking sheet; set aside. Toast 125 g/4 oz blanched whole or flaked almonds under a hot grill, tossing

them occasionally, until straw blond. Stir into the hot caramel, pour on to the prepared baking sheet and leave to set. When hard, break into pieces and keep in an airtight jar until ready to use.

To crush, place in a polythene bag and crush with a rolling pin. Makes 225 g/8 oz.

Hazelnut Brittle or Praline: Lightly oil a baking sheet; set aside. Toast 125 g/4 oz whole hazelnuts under a hot grill for 3–4 minutes, then rub them in a clean tea towel to remove the skins. Stir the nuts into the hot caramel, pour on to the prepared baking sheet and leave to set. When hard, break into pieces. Store in an airtight jar. Makes 225 g/8 oz.

Caramel Sauce: Measure 120 ml/4 fl oz water into a cup and set aside.

Prepare caramel as above, using 275 g/10 oz sugar, to golden mahogany liquid, then remove pan from heat. Immediately holding the spoon by the extreme end and, standing well back, carefully pour in the measured water and stir carefully: this will cause a brief burst of steam. Return the caramel to the heat and simmer, stirring until a smooth sauce is formed. Use to flavour mousses, creams and custards, or serve with ice cream. Makes 200 ml/7 fl oz.

Caramel coated fruits – such as strawberries, grapes and mandarin segments – are delicious.

Butterscotch Sauce: Measure 3 tbsp double cream and 25 g/1 oz unsalted butter into separate bowls and set aside. Prepare caramel as above, but use 125 g/4 oz sugar, to golden mahogany liquid. Remove from the heat and carefully stir in the cream and butter all at once. Continue stirring until even. Use to flavour custards, mousses and creams, to pour over ice cream or to top sponge puddings. Makes 175 ml/6 fl oz.

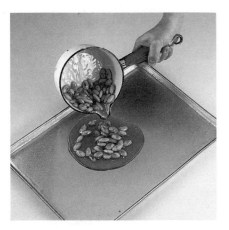

Chocolate Mousse with Hazelnut Praline

WATCHPOINTS

◆

Caramel ◆ Meringue

SERVES 6–8

200 g/7 oz best quality plain
   chocolate

3 eggs, at room temperature,
   separated

2 tbsp caster sugar

75 g/3 oz hazelnut brittle (page 69)

275 ml/10 fl oz double cream, softly
   whipped

To decorate:

150 ml/5 fl oz whipping cream

50 g/2 oz hazelnut brittle (page 69),
   broken (optional)

Open a box of chocolates, pass them around and I doubt very much whether there will be a hazelnut praline left. Flavour a dark chocolate mousse with hazelnut praline and it too will disappear with similar gusto.

———— ◆ ————

Break the chocolate into a bowl, place over a saucepan of simmering water and allow to melt slowly, 2–3 minutes. It is important not to get any moisture or steam near the chocolate or it may thicken and become grainy. Remove from the heat and stir in the egg yolks.

Place the egg whites in a large mixing bowl. Whisk until they will hold their weight on the whisk. Add the sugar and continue whisking until soft peaks will form. Fold the chocolate mixture into the egg whites together with the crushed brittle. Add the whipped cream and fold in evenly.

Turn the mousse into individual serving dishes and decorate with whipped cream and pieces of broken brittle, if liked. Serve cold.

Illustrated on page 67

Crème Caramel

WATCHPOINTS

◆

Caramel ◆ Egg Custard

SERVES 8

2 tbsp water

225 g/8 oz caster sugar

850 ml/1½ pints milk

½ tsp vanilla essence

6 eggs

Just a glimpse of the dark caramel pooling round this dessert will set the mind to rehearsing the graceful motion of a spoon carving its way effortlessly through the irresistible custard. The finely grated zest of 1 orange may be added to the milk, or 75 g/3 oz best quality plain chocolate melted in the milk, for new flavours.

———— ◆ ————

Preheat the oven to 180°C/350°F/gas 4. Place 8 dariole moulds or a 1 litre/2 pint soufflé dish in a deep roasting pan.

To prepare the caramel, measure the 2 tbsp cold water into a cup and set aside. Put 2 tbsp of the sugar into a heavy saucepan and melt over a moderate heat, stirring, until beginning to brown. Continue to add a further 125 g/4 oz of sugar, a little at a time, stirring continuously to dissolve, then allow to caramelize to a mahogany brown colour.

Remove from the heat, stand well back and add the water. There will be a sudden burst of steam, but this will die down quickly. Stir until even, then pour the hot caramel into the moulds or mould and set aside.

To prepare the custard, put the milk and vanilla essence in a heavy saucepan and bring to the boil. Lightly beat the eggs with the remaining sugar in a bowl. Pour the boiling milk over the eggs, stirring well. Strain into the prepared moulds.

Add boiling water to the roasting pan to come halfway up the sides of the moulds and cover with a baking sheet. Bake in the preheated oven for 25–30 minutes or until a knife inserted in the centre of the custards will come away cleanly. Allow to cool, then chill. To serve, run a wetted finger around the edge of the custard and shake from side to side to release.

Illustrated on page 66

Walnut Sponge Pudding with Butterscotch

WATCHPOINTS
♦
Caramel ♦ Classic Sponge Cake

SERVES 6–8

150 g/5 oz soft butter, plus a little extra for greasing
1 recipe butterscotch sauce (page 69)
125 g/4 oz shelled walnuts
150 g/5 oz caster sugar
2 eggs, at room temperature, beaten
150 g/5 oz self-raising flour

During the cold weather there are few things that warm the cockles of the heart in quite the same way as a steamed sponge pudding, especially when it is served with lashings of piping hot custard. Deliciously rich, moist and moreish, this recipe features a stunning walnut sponge topped with a homemade butterscotch sauce.

♦

Lightly grease a 1.1 litre/2 pint pudding basin with soft butter. Place one third of the butterscotch sauce and half of the walnuts in the bottom and set aside. Chop the rest of the walnuts.

Place the soft butter and sugar in a mixing bowl and beat together until pale and fluffy. Add the eggs a little at a time and beat until smooth. Stir in the flour and walnuts.

Turn the mixture into the prepared pudding basin and cover with a circle of greaseproof paper. Cover the basin with a piece of foil and secure.

To steam the pudding, stand basin in a large saucepan, add 7.5 cm/3 inches water and bring to the boil. Cover and steam for 1 hour 15 minutes, topping up water as necessary. To serve, remove foil and turn out on to a serving dish. Spoon over the remaining butterscotch sauce.

Illustrated on page 66

Butterscotch Pecan Tart

SERVES 6

1 recipe rich biscuit pastry (page 139)

75 g/3 oz caster sugar

3 tbsp maple syrup or golden syrup

4 tbsp double cream

50 g/2 oz unsalted butter

225 g/8 oz shelled pecan or walnut halves

One of the most delicious ways with butterscotch, this tart can also be made with walnuts.

———— ◆ ————

Roll out the pastry on a lightly floured surface to a thickness of 6 mm/¼ inch and use to line a 20 cm/8 inch flan tin evenly. Preheat the oven to 190°C/375°F/gas 5.

The prepare the filling, place the sugar and syrup in a heavy saucepan over a moderate heat, stirring occasionally, until the sugar has dissolved. Increase the heat and boil rapidly for 5 minutes or until lightly caramelized. Remove from the heat and stir in the cream and butter until evenly mixed. Stir in the pecan or walnut halves and turn into pastry case. (The heat of the mixture will not harm the pastry.)

Bake in the centre of the preheated oven for 25–30 minutes. Allow to cool, and serve with whipped cream.

Sliced Oranges in a Caramel Sauce

SERVES 4

4 oranges

150 g/5 oz caster sugar

2 tbsp water

Scrub the oranges with warm soapy water to remove the waxy veneer and rinse well. Pare the zest from two of the oranges with a vegetable peeler, avoiding the bitter white pith; cut into thin strips. Place in a saucepan of water and simmer for 3–4 minutes until tender; drain.

Cut the top and bottom from each orange with a serrated knife. Stand each orange on a flat end and cut away the peel from top to bottom, removing all pith. Slice the oranges into rounds and arrange in a serving dish.

To prepare the caramel, melt 2 tbsp of the sugar in a heavy saucepan over low heat, stirring. Continue to add the sugar a little at a time, stirring to dissolve, then allow to caramelize to a light golden colour.

Remove from the heat, stand well back and add the water. Stir until even, then add the orange zest and pour over the sliced oranges. Allow to cool before serving.

Sliced oranges in a Caramel Sauce; Butterscotch Pecan Tart

Frankfurter Kranz

WATCHPOINTS
◆
Caramel ◆ Classic Sponge Cake ◆ Crème Pâtissière

SERVES 6–8

Sponge:

175 g/6 oz soft unsalted butter, plus
a little extra for greasing

175 g/6 oz caster sugar

3 eggs, at room temperature, beaten

175 g/6 oz self-raising flour

Syrup:

3 tbsp golden syrup

150 ml/5 fl oz boiling water

2 tbsp Kirsch or Grand Marnier

To finish:

1 recipe crème diplomat (page 27)

1 recipe almond praline (page 69),
crushed

8 candied mimosa

candied angelica strips

No, it's not a hotdog nor does it belong in a bun. Frankfurter Kranz is a delicious sponge baked in an angel cake tin, moistened with a Kirsch syrup, layered with crème diplomat and masked with crushed praline.

———— ◆ ————

Preheat the oven to 180°C/350°F/gas 4. Grease a 20 cm/8 inch angel cake tin and dust with flour.

To make the sponge, beat the butter and sugar together until pale and fluffy. Add eggs a little at a time and beat until smooth. Fold in the flour.

Turn into the prepared tin and bake in the centre of the preheated oven for 40–45 minutes or until a skewer inserted into the centre comes away cleanly. Turn out on to a wire rack to cool.

Slice the cake into three layers. Combine the syrup ingredients together and use to moisten each cake layer. Sandwich the layers together with crème diplomat. Cover the cake with the remaining crème diplomat and press on the crushed praline. Decorate with candied mimosa and angelica.

Frankfurter Kranz;
Caramelized Apple
Sponge Cake.

Caramelized Apple Sponge Cake

WATCHPOINTS
◆
Caramel ◆ Whisked Sponge

SERVES 6

soft butter for greasing

75 g/3 oz butter

900 g/2 lb dessert apples, peeled,
quartered and cored

4 tbsp caster sugar

2 tbsp water

Sponge:

3 eggs, size 2–3, at room
temperature

75 g/3 oz caster sugar

75 g/3 oz plain flour

Lightly grease a 20 cm/8 inch cake tin. Line the base with greaseproof paper and dust the sides with flour. Preheat the oven to 190°C/375°F/gas 5.

Melt half of the butter in a large frying pan, add the apples and toss in the butter for 6–8 minutes until golden. Spoon into the bottom of the cake tin.

Dissolve sugar in water in frying pan, then simmer until it begins to caramelize, 4–5 minutes. Stir in remaining butter and pour over apples.

To prepare the sponge, whisk the eggs and sugar together in a mixing bowl until the mixture is thick enough to leave a lasting ribbon across the surface, 3–4 minutes. Sift the flour over and fold in with a metal spoon.

Pour the sponge mixture over the apples. Bake in the centre of the preheated oven for 30–35 minutes. To serve, run a knife around the edge of the cake, invert on to a serving dish and serve hot, with custard sauce.

'Talking of pleasure, this moment I am writing with one hand, with the other holding to my mouth a nectarine – good God, how fine. It went down all pulpy, slushy, oozy – it's embonpoint melted down my throat like a large beautified strawberry. I shall certainly breed.'

JOHN KEATS, letter to Charles Dilke, 22 September 1819.

Fresh fruit is the most valuable source of inspiration available to the creative dessert cook. In my kitchen I keep on display a basket of whatever fruits I find in season. As I write it is late autumn and my basket is brimming with apples, oranges and pears. I chose them because they were inexpensive and in perfect condition. Oddly enough, apart from their visual appeal, fruits that are in season tend also to have complementary flavours. When the fruits in my basket are in accordance with the season, I can be reassured that a successful dessert, however simple, is in the offing.

If, when we are deciding which fruits will work best together, we also try to think of combining them with meringue, egg custard, crème pâtissière, caramel or any of the sponges or pastries in this book, we will, without doubt, be inspired with new and exciting ideas for desserts. The best ideas are often the most simple, and nine times out of ten they are not inspired by old recipe books but by that ever-changing, ever-promising basket of fruit. Try poaching

6

Mouthwatering

Fruit Desserts

pears, apricots or other fruit in a light syrup and serving with yogurt or fromage frais, for example.

Some fruits – like Keats' mouth-watering nectarine – hardly need improving and are best eaten and enjoyed just as they are. Yet often a touch of vanilla, a blob of cream or a splash of alcohol will enhance the flavour of fruit. Why settle for strawberries as they are when you can soak them in port and Grand Marnier and serve them with crème fraîche? It is these discoveries which have gradually evolved into classic dessert combinations.

When buying fruit, always choose the finest produce available and never settle for second best. To enjoy fruit, it must be in optimum condition – and perfectly ripe. Don't be afraid to complain to your greengrocer or supermarket about the quality of the fruit if necessary. After all, if we refuse to buy rubbish, eventually they will stop selling it.

Whenever there is an abundance of soft fruit to be had, there are always delicious sauces to be made, all of which can be frozen without harming flavour. Fresh fruit sauces will keep in the refrigerator for up to 5 days, and find themselves poured over anything from vanilla ice cream to meringues, fruit flans and tarts. Soft fruit purées are an ideal way to make use of a plentiful crop of berry fruits as they can be frozen successfully for up to 6 months, and used as a basis for fresh fruit sauces and toppings.

Excellent sauces can be made from frozen raspberries, strawberries, blackcurrants and blackberries. Even a can of apricots, mangoes or gooseberries can be whizzed up in the blender or food processor with their own juices to make a tempting quick sauce. So indispensable are fruit sauces to the creative cook, that I have included several in this section.

A particularly delicious way of serving fresh fruits in season is to enclose them with appropriate flavourings in fine, delicate crêpes. To introduce this section of fruit desserts I have therefore chosen subtly spiced apple and pear crêpes as the master recipe.

Illustrated overleaf: Fruit Salad with Rum and Mango Sauce; Spiced Apple and Pear Crêpes; Strawberry Shortcake; Summer Pudding.

fragrant, fruity

& Sauces

1

Seasonal fruits have the best flavour and are often the least expensive. Select the best quality available.

2

If your chosen fruit is perfectly ripe, do not be tempted to improve it further. Rather serve it as simply as possible and enjoy its natural flavour to the full.

3

A particular enzyme is present in uncooked pineapple, mango, guava and other tropical fruits which prevents the setting action of gelatine. If you wish to use any of these fruits to flavour mousses or jellies, the fruits must first be poached in a light syrup to neutralize this enzyme.

4

Lemon juice contains citric acid which helps to prevent discoloration of certain fruits. Vitamin C – ascorbic acid – can be used instead of lemon juice and is most effective when poaching apples, pears, plums and cherries in syrup. Use one 50 mg Vitamin C tablet to every 1 litre/1^3/$_4$ pints of light syrup.

5

To remove the skins from peaches, nectarines and apricots, blanch in boiling water for 2–3 minutes until the skins split and loosen. Refresh in cold water to prevent softening. Peaches, nectarines and apricots that are picked underripe and have been allowed to ripen in transit are often difficult to peel; unfortunately this is impossible to detect.

6

When preparing soft fruit purées, use stainless steel or enamel saucepans. Avoid contact with aluminium, steel and unlined copper as these react with acid fruits, adversely affecting the flavour.

7

Always use a fine nylon sieve to sieve soft fruit purées.

8

Grated lemon and orange rinds are often used to impart flavour. Before grating the rind, wash the fruit thoroughly in warm soapy water to remove the waxy veneer. Rinse and dry well.

Crêpes are an excellent choice for dessert – they cost next to nothing, are easy to make and can be filled with delicious confections of fruit, custard and cream.

Apples and pears are beautifully enhanced by ground cinnamon, ginger and allspice in this quick, easy filling.

If you are planning ahead, the crêpes can be filled, arranged in a serving dish and put to one side. When ready to serve, they can be warmed through in the oven.

SERVES 4
soft butter for greasing

Crêpes:
100 g/4 oz plain flour
275 ml/^{1}/$_2$ pint milk
2 eggs
1 tbsp caster sugar
1 tsp vegetable oil
butter or oil for frying, if necessary

Filling:
25 g/1 oz butter
450 g/1 lb dessert apples, peeled, cored and roughly chopped
450 g/1 lb pears, peeled, cored and roughly chopped
^{1}/$_2$ tsp ground cinnamon
^{1}/$_2$ tsp ground ginger
1 pinch ground allspice or cloves
2 tbsp caster sugar or more to taste

To serve:
icing sugar for dusting

1 To make the crêpe batter, measure the flour into a mixing bowl and make a well in the centre. Add about half of the milk and stir into a firm, lump-free batter.

Add the remaining milk, the eggs and sugar, and beat well to make a smooth batter, the consistency of single cream. Stir in the oil. If you have time it is preferable to leave the batter to stand for an hour or so: the crêpes will be lighter and all the more delicious.

2 To make the crêpes, heat an 18 cm/7 inch diameter non-stick frying pan over a steady heat. (It will not be necessary to oil a non-stick pan, but you will have to grease a pan without a non-stick finish.) Transfer the batter to a jug and pour enough batter into the heated pan just to coat the bottom, tilting until even. Allow 30 seconds for the crêpe to brown on the underside, then turn

it over and cook briefly until lightly coloured on the second side.

Continue making the remaining crêpes in the same way. If the batter seems to be a little too thick, thin it down with milk or water until the correct consistency is reached. As they are cooked, stack the crêpes on a plate and cover with foil.

3 Preheat the oven to 190°C/375°F/gas 5. Lightly grease a 23 cm/9 inch square shallow ovenproof dish with soft butter and set aside.

4 To prepare the filling, melt the butter in a heavy saucepan until it bubbles and begins to brown. Add the apples, pears and spices and stir together. Cover the saucepan and cook gently for 3–4 minutes until the apples soften without completely falling apart. Add sugar to taste.

5 Place the crêpes, two at a time, on the work surface, spoon the filling across each and roll up. Arrange side by side in the dish.

Cover the dish with foil and warm through in the preheated oven for 20–25 minutes. Serve with vanilla ice cream, pouring cream or custard.

VARIATIONS

Wholemeal Crêpes: Replace the plain flour with wholemeal and add a little extra liquid.

Apricot and Apple Crêpes: Use fresh or canned apricots instead of the pears and omit the spices.

Blackberry and Almond Crêpes: Make crêpes as above. For filling stir 400 g/14 oz drained, stoned canned black cherries into 1 recipe frangipan sponge mixture (page 101). Fill crêpes and bake as above. Dust with icing sugar and serve with ice cream.

Apricot Sauce

MAKES 400 ml/14 fl oz
350 g/12 oz fresh apricots
150 ml/5 fl oz water
3 tbsp granulated sugar

When I started my apprenticeship as a young pâtissier in London, I worked under an old Dutch chef called Ray. Apart from teaching me the finer points of pastry-making, he took great delight in telling me how to charm the girls. According to Ray, you can tell a nice girl not by her looks but by her affection for apricots. When, he said, you have won her over, keep her supplied with apricots, baked as they may be in tarts or with custard, and her happiness will be yours for as long as you wish. As you can imagine, Ray was a bit of a joker, but I have since discovered an element of truth regarding apricots. This sauce will nearly always do the trick, poured over vanilla ice cream, apple tarts and almond sponge puddings.

———————— ◆ ————————

Cut the apricots in half, remove the stones and place the apricot halves in a stainless steel or enamel saucepan with the water and sugar. Cover and simmer for 6–8 minutes. Allow to cool slightly, then rub through a fine nylon sieve. Chill well before serving.

VARIATION
Use 400 g/14 oz canned whole apricots in syrup. Stone the apricots, then put into a food processor or blender with the syrup and whizz to a smooth purée. Serve chilled.

Blackcurrant Sauce

MAKES 225 ml/8 fl oz
175 g/6 oz blackcurrants, fresh,
    frozen or canned
150 ml/5 fl oz plus 1 tbsp water
50 g/2 oz granulated sugar
2 tsp cornflour

The powerful colour and flavour of blackcurrants lend themselves perfectly to sharp sauces and toppings, and a host of other fruit desserts. The blackcurrant enhances the flavour of many fruits – apples, pears, peaches, melons, papaya or paw paw and mango. Blackcurrant sauce is also delicious poured over a dish of vanilla ice cream and meringues.

———————— ◆ ————————

Measure the blackcurrants into a stainless steel or enamel saucepan together with 150 ml/5 fl oz of the water and the sugar. If using canned blackcurrants, use the juice instead of water. Cover the saucepan and simmer for 3–4 minutes or until the berries have burst.

Slake the cornflour with the remaining water, stir into the sauce and simmer to thicken. Sieve, then allow to cool before serving.

Raspberry Sauce

MAKES 275 ml/10 fl oz
350 g/12 oz raspberries,
    fresh or frozen
3 tbsp granulated sugar

Raspberry sauce is particularly delicious poured over fresh peaches, figs and mangoes. It is also called Melba Sauce.

———————— ◆ ————————

Put the raspberries and sugar into a stainless steel or enamel saucepan, cover and simmer over a low heat for 6–8 minutes until the juices have run. Allow the fruit to cool, then rub through a fine nylon sieve. Make sure that the pips are rubbed clean before discarding them. Chill before serving.

Strawberry Sauce

MAKES 275 ml/10 fl oz
350 g/12 oz strawberries,
    fresh or frozen
2 tbsp icing sugar
finely grated zest and juice of
    ½ orange
2 tbsp Kirsch or
    Grand Marnier

Contrary to what many people think, the flavour of strawberries is in fact limited in its ability to enhance or complement other fruits, but there is no doubt that it is perfect with fresh pineapple and orange. Try this special sauce spooned over slices of fresh pineapple.

———————— ◆ ————————

Hull the strawberries, put them in a food processor or blender with the other ingredients and purée. Pass the purée through a fine nylon sieve to remove the pips, and chill before serving.

Rum and Mango Sauce

MAKES 425 ml/15 fl oz
1 large ripe mango
2 tbsp light brown soft sugar
125 ml/4 fl oz water
3 tbsp dark rum

Fresh mangoes are especially delicious made into a smooth sauce, spiked with dark rum, to pour over a salad of pineapple, banana, papaya, lychees and raspberries. If you cannot get fresh mangoes, make an agreeable sauce by blending a can of mangoes with the juice of a lemon and a dash of rum.

———————— ◆ ————————

Remove the top and bottom from the mango with a serrated knife, stand the mango up on one end and cut away the skin. Cut the flesh away from either side of the stone and chop roughly.

Measure the brown sugar and water into a saucepan and bring to the boil, stirring until dissolved. Place the mango in a food processor or blender and purée. Add the syrup and rum. Chill well before serving.

Hot Chocolate, Rum and Banana Crêpes

WATCHPOINTS
– ◆ –
Fruit

SERVES 4

1 recipe crêpe batter (see recipe)

2 tbsp cocoa powder

1 tbsp caster sugar

Filling:

3 ripe bananas, sliced

2 tbsp dark rum

1 tbsp soft brown sugar

finely grated zest and juice
of ¹/₂ orange

To decorate:

icing sugar for dusting

orange rind shreds (blanched)

Chocolate crêpes are absolutely delicious served hot with bananas, rum and ice cream.

———— ◆ ————

Make the crêpe batter (as described on page 81), replacing 2 tbsp of the flour with the cocoa powder and adding the additional 1 tbsp caster sugar. Make 8 crêpes. Keep warm.

To prepare the filling, put the bananas into a stainless steel or enamel saucepan and add the rum, sugar, orange zest and juice. Warm over a gentle heat until the bananas are just begining to soften, 2–3 minutes.

Divide the filling between the crêpes, fold in half and dust with sifted icing sugar. Decorate with orange rind shreds. Serve immediately, with coffee or vanilla ice cream.

Flaming Hot Bananas
with Jamaica Rum and Orange

WATCHPOINTS
– ◆ –
Fruit

SERVES 4

8 ripe bananas

4 tbsp caster sugar

¹/₂ vanilla pod or ¹/₂ tsp vanilla
essence

finely grated zest and juice
of 1 orange

4 tbsp dark rum

The idea for this dessert came during the winter when all I had in my fruit basket was a bunch of ripe bananas and an orange.

———— ◆ ————

Preheat the oven to 200°C/400°F/gas 6. Peel the bananas, halve them crossways and arrange in a baking dish.

Place 1 tbsp of the sugar in a mortar. Split open the vanilla pod down the middle with a small knife and scrape out the fine black paste. Add this – or the vanilla essence – to the sugar with the grated orange zest and mix together using a pestle. Add the remaining sugar and distribute between the bananas.

Combine half of the rum with the orange juice and pour over the bananas. Cover the dish tightly with foil and bake in the centre of the preheated oven for 20–25 minutes. When ready to serve, warm the remaining rum in a ladle, ignite and pour over the bananas. When the flames have died down, serve the bananas with Greek yogurt or ice cream.

Hot Chocolate, Rum and Banana Crêpes; Flaming Hot Bananas with Jamaica Rum and Orange.

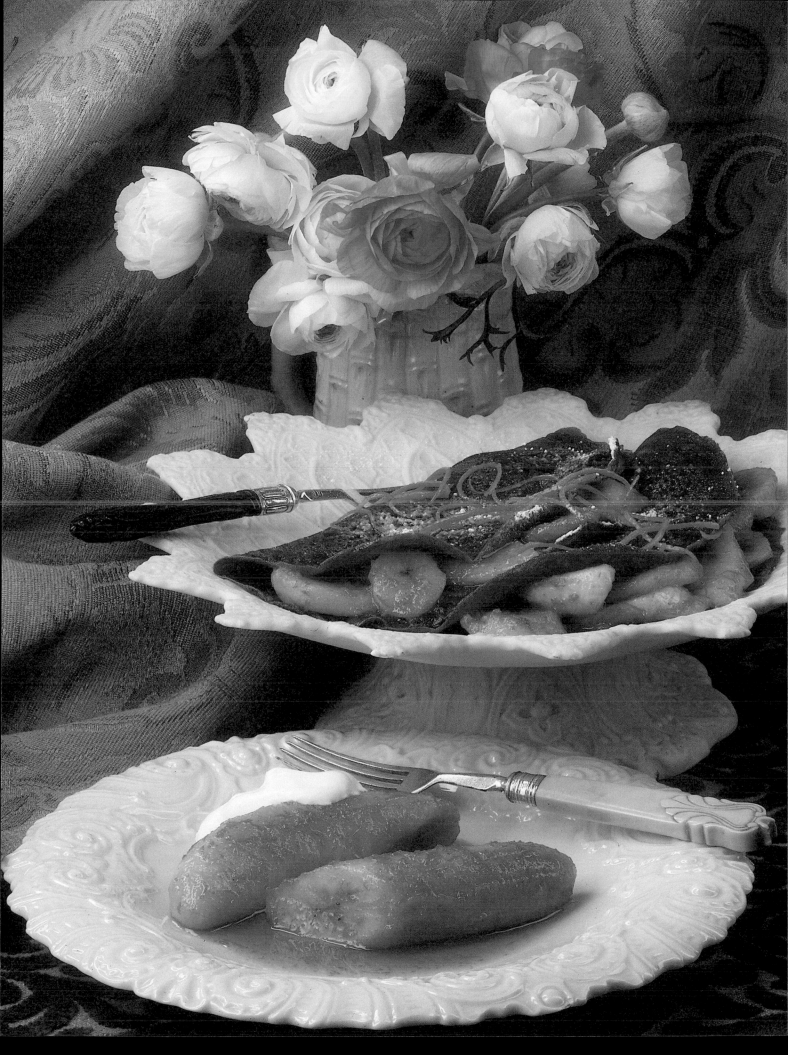

Poires Belle Hélène

WATCHPOINTS
– ◆ –
Fruit

SERVES 4

850 ml/1¹/₂ pints water

175 g/6 oz granulated sugar

juice of ¹/₂ lemon, or two 50 mg
    vitamin C tablets

1 vanilla pod, or 1 tsp vanilla essence

4 dessert pears

Hot chocolate sauce:

150 ml/5 fl oz single cream or milk

1 tbsp caster sugar

175 g/6 oz best quality plain
    chocolate, chopped

To finish:

1 litre/1³/₄ pints vanilla ice cream
    (page 53)

50 g/2 oz flaked almonds, toasted

For this stunningly simple dessert we owe our gratitude to the master chef Georges Auguste Escoffier who created it originally as a lady's dessert. Poires Belle Hélène consists of a poached pear served with vanilla ice cream and hot chocolate sauce to create a delicious contrast.

———————— ◆ ————————

Measure the water and sugar into a saucepan, add the lemon juice or vitamin C tablets and vanilla and bring to the boil. Leave to simmer while you peel the pears. Peel the pears from top to bottom with a vegetable peeler and scoop out the inside cores with a melon scoop, working from the bases. Place the pears in the syrup, cover with a circle of greaseproof paper and simmer for 20–25 minutes or until tender. Allow to cool, then chill.

To make the chocolate sauce put the cream or milk and sugar into a heavy saucepan and bring to the boil. Remove from the heat, add the chocolate and stir until melted.

To serve, scoop the vanilla ice cream into individual dishes and stand a pear in each. Pour the hot chocolate sauce over and sprinkle with almonds.

Clafoutis

SERVES 4

2 tbsp plain flour

2 tbsp caster sugar

1 good pinch ground cinnamon

225 ml/8 fl oz milk

2 eggs

1 tbsp Kirsch or Cognac (optional)

450 g/1 lb fresh tart black cherries,
    or 450 g/1 lb bottled black
    cherries

soft butter for greasing

icing sugar for dusting

This simple French dessert is made by baking a layer of dark cherries in a pancake batter until crisp and golden.

———————— ◆ ————————

To prepare the batter, place the flour, sugar and cinnamon in a bowl. Add one third of the milk and stir to a smooth paste. Add the remaining milk with the eggs and, if using, the Kirsch or Cognac. Allow to stand for 30–40 minutes before using.

Preheat the oven to 190°C/375°F/gas 5. Stone the cherries and arrange in a single layer in a lightly greased gratin dish. Pour the batter over to three-quarters cover the cherries. Bake in the preheated oven for 40–45 minutes. Dust with sifted icing sugar, and serve warm or cold, with cream.

Poires Belle Hélène; Clafoutis.

Vanilla Pears with an Almond Filling

SERVES 4

850 ml/1½ pints water

175 g/6 oz granulated sugar

juice of ½ lemon, or two 50 mg
    vitamin C tablets

1 vanilla pod, or 1 tsp vanilla essence

4 dessert pears

Almond filling:

1 tbsp Grand Marnier

75 g/3 oz white marzipan

25 g/1 oz almond macaroons,
    crushed

To decorate:

25 g/1 oz flaked almonds, toasted

Eating this dessert for the first time, one could be forgiven for suspecting little more than ordinary poached pears, but as your spoon carves its way through the cool vanilla-scented flesh you will discover that buried inside is a filling so delicious that there do not exist words to describe it.

———————— ◆ ————————

Put the water, sugar, lemon juice or Vitamin C and vanilla in a saucepan and bring to a simmer. Peel the pears and remove the inside cores with a melon scoop, working from the bases. Place the pears in the syrup, cover with a circle of greaseproof paper and poach gently for 20–25 minutes or until tender, then leave to cool in the syrup.

To prepare the filling, work the Grand Marnier into the marzipan until softened and smooth. Mix in the crushed macaroons.

Drain the cooled pears, reserving syrup, and push a little filling into each one; chill. Serve the pears in a pool of syrup, decorated with almonds.

Brandied Peaches in a Zabaglione Cream

SERVES 6

4 large peaches

25 g/1 oz butter, preferably unsalted

1 tbsp brandy

Zabaglione cream:

1 egg

2 egg yolks

2 tbsp caster sugar

2 tbsp brandy

The idea for this dessert came during a last-minute panic when all I had at my disposal were a few peaches, some eggs and a bottle of brandy.

———————— ◆ ————————

Place the peaches in a large bowl, cover with boiling water and leave for 20–30 seconds to loosen the skins. Drain the peaches and plunge into cold water, then peel. Cut the peaches into large slices.

Melt the butter in a large frying pan until it begins to foam. Add the peaches and toss in the butter until they begin to brown. Stir in the brandy and transfer to individual flameproof dishes.

Preheat the grill to medium-high. Place all of the zabaglione ingredients in a bowl over a pan of boiling water. Whisk until the mixture is thick enough to hold its weight on the whisk, 3–4 minutes using an electric whisk set at the lowest speed.

Spoon the zabaglione over the peaches and grill for 6–8 minutes until golden. Serve immediately.

Vanilla Pears with an Almond Filling; Brandied Peaches in a Zabaglione Cream.

Pêches Rafraîchis Bourguignonne

WATCHPOINTS
– ◆ –
Fruit

SERVES 4

450 g/1 lb raspberries, fresh or frozen

175 ml/6 fl oz Beaujolais or other
    fruity red wine

3 tbsp icing sugar

8 ripe peaches

To decorate:

raspberries or raspberry leaves

50 g/2 oz flaked almonds, toasted
    (optional)

Bring me some beautifully ripe peaches, some sweet-scented raspberries and a bottle of Beaujolais wine and I will show you how to prepare one of the most talked-about desserts this side of the crème brûlée.

———— ◆ ————

Purée the raspberries in a blender then rub through a nylon sieve into a bowl. Stir in the wine and icing sugar.

Place the peaches in a large bowl, cover with boiling water and leave for 20–30 seconds. Drain the peaches, plunge into cold water, then peel. Slice into the sauce and leave to macerate for $1^{1}/_{2}$-2 hours, or longer. Serve decorated with raspberries or leaves, and flaked almonds if desired.

Frozen Pineapple and Orange Soufflé; Pêches Refraîchis Bourguignonne.

Frozen Pineapple and Orange Soufflé

WATCHPOINTS
———— ◆ ————
Whisked Sponge ◆ Fruit

SERVES 8

4 oranges

4 small macaroons or sponge fingers
    (page 101), coarsely crumbled

2 tbsp dark rum

3 eggs, at room temperature

150 g/5 oz caster sugar

2 tsp powdered gelatine

1 tbsp cold water

275 ml/10 fl oz double cream, softly
    whipped

75 g/3 oz pineapple, cored and
    crushed or finely chopped

Cut a piece of stiff paper to fit around the edge of a 15 cm/6 inch soufflé dish so as to raise the edge by 5 cm/2 inches and secure with freezer tape.

Scrub two of the oranges with warm soapy water and rinse well to remove their waxy veneer, then grate the zest finely. Peel and segment these oranges; reserve for decoration. Remove the peel and pith from the other two oranges and roughly chop the flesh.

Soak the macaroons or sponge fingers in the rum.

Whisk the eggs and sugar together until thick enough to leave a lasting ribbon across the surface. Soften the gelatine in the cold water, then dissolve over a pan of boiling water. Add to the egg mixture and whisk in the grated orange zest. Fold in the cream, then gently stir in the chopped orange and pineapple together with the rum-soaked macaroons.

Pile the mixture into the prepared soufflé dish and freeze for $2^{1}/_{2}$-3 hours. Test with a knife to ensure the soufflé is soft enough to serve.

To serve, remove the paper collar from the dish and decorate the soufflé with orange segments.

Strawberries Romanoff

SERVES 6
900 g/2 lb strawberries, hulled
225 ml/8 fl oz orange juice
125 g /4 fl oz ruby port
50 ml/2 fl oz Grand Marnier
2 tbsp caster sugar
275 ml/10 fl oz double cream
1 tbsp icing sugar

I once thought the best way to enjoy strawberies was to dip them in caster sugar and devour them with cream. I was wrong. Delicious though they are, these fruits assume heavenly proportions when they have taken up the flavours of port and Grand Marnier. Serve them with a strawberry cream sauce and you will wonder what has hit you.

———————— ◆ ————————

Place 175 g/6 oz of the largest strawberries in a blender and purée until smooth. Place the remainder in a bowl and pour over the orange juice, port, Grand Marnier and sugar. Stir gently, then leave to macerate in the refrigerator for at least 2 hours.

For the sauce, softly whip the cream with the icing sugar. Stir in the strawberry purée. To serve, lift the strawberries out of their liquid into glass serving dishes and spoon over the cream sauce.

Illustrated on page 94

Summer Pudding

SERVES 6
8–10 slices thin white bread, crusts
    removed
225 ml/8 fl oz water
50 g/2 oz granulated sugar
125 g/4 oz black cherries, stoned
125 g/4 oz blackcurrants, stripped
    from their stalks
125 g/4 oz redcurrants, stripped
    from their stalks
125 g/4 oz strawberries, hulled
125 g/4 oz raspberries
125 g/4 oz blackberries
2 tsp powdered gelatine
extra soft fruits to decorate

The English summer is almost a contradiction in terms, since it is difficult — even for the Englishman — to determine when, if at all, summer occurs. Is it the warmest day, or the day it chose not to rain, or is it that brief moment, usually during August, when berry fruits are at their ripest and we can put together a delicious summer pudding? It isn't essential to have all the fruits listed, but the total weight should be 700 g/1½ lb.

———————— ◆ ————————

Line the bottom and sides of a 1.1 litre/2 pint pudding basin with overlapping slices of bread, reserving two slices for the lid.

Put 200 ml/7 fl oz of the water and the sugar in a saucepan and bring to the boil, stirring to dissolve. Simmer the cherries in the syrup for 8 minutes, then transfer with a slotted spoon to a nylon sieve set over a bowl. Add the rest of the fruit to the syrup, return to the heat and simmer for 3 minutes. Add the fruit to the cherries and leave to drain.

Mix the fruits together and fill the lined basin to the top. Add the juices in the bowl to the syrup.

Soften the gelatine in the remaining 2 tbsp water, then stir into the warm fruit syrup to dissolve. Pour one third of the syrup over the pudding. Cover with the reserved bread slices and top with a saucer. Weight down and leave the pudding in the refrigerator overnight to become firm.

To serve the summer pudding, run a table knife around the inside of the basin, invert a serving dish over the basin and turn the right way up. If the pudding remains stubbornly in the basin, try dipping the base into hot water for the count of 10. Brush the pudding with the reserved syrup, decorate with soft fruit and serve with whipped cream or yogurt.

Illustrated on page 79

Strawberry Shortcake

WATCHPOINTS
— ◆ —
Fruit

SERVES 6

Shortcake:

250 g/9 oz plain flour

175 g/6 oz cool butter, cut into pieces

75 g/3 oz caster sugar, plus extra for sprinkling

Filling:

450 g/1 lb strawberries

275 ml/10 fl oz double cream

1 tbsp caster sugar

Strawberry shortcake caters perfectly for the unexpected guest. The shortcakes can be made well in advance and stored away in a biscuit tin. As your guests arrive, simply sandwich the crisp shortcake layers with strawberries and whipped cream.

———— ◆ ————

Preheat the oven to 180°C/350°F/gas 4. For the shortcake, put the flour, butter and sugar into a mixing bowl and rub together with the fingertips until the mixture resembles large breadcrumbs. Alternatively, use a food processor. Push the mixture together with the fingers to form a short pastry, and divide into three equal portions.

Press or roll out each portion on a lightly greased baking sheet to a 20 cm/8 inch round. Crimp the edges to form an attractive border, sprinkle with caster sugar and prick the surface with a fork. Bake in the preheated oven for 20 minutes. Allow to cool.

To assemble the shortcake, whip the cream with the sugar until thick. Sandwich the layers together with cream and strawberries, covering the top with an arrangement of strawberries.

Illustrated on page 79

Blueberry Cheesecake

SERVES 8

75 g/3 oz unsalted butter
175 g/6 oz semi-sweet biscuits
1 tbsp powdered gelatine
2 tbsp cold water
350 g/12 oz full fat soft cheese
275 ml/10 fl oz plain yogurt
75 g/3 oz caster sugar
3 egg whites, at room temperature
150 ml/5 fl oz whipping cream,
    whipped until thick
350 g/12 oz blueberries

Glaze:
175 ml/6 fl oz water
2 tbsp caster sugar
1 tbsp arrowroot

Cheesecakes are a popular finish to any meal and are especially attractive when decorated with seasonal fruits. This basic recipe may be adapted to use any number of summer fruits as a delicious topping.

——————— ♦ ———————

Grease a 20 cm/8 inch loose-bottomed cake tin. Line the bottom with a round of greaseproof paper and the sides with a narrow strip.

Melt the butter in a small saucepan. Finely crush the biscuits in a polythene bag, using a rolling pin, and stir into the melted butter. Spread the crumbs over the bottom of the cake tin and press down into an even layer with the back of a spoon. Set aside.

Sprinkle the gelatine into a small cup or bowl containing the cold water. Leave to soften for a few minutes, then stand the bowl in a saucepan of simmering water and stir until the gelatine has completely dissolved.

Place the soft cheese, yogurt and 25 g/1 oz of the sugar in a mixing bowl and blend together until even. Whisk the egg whites in a large clean bowl until they will hold their weight on the whisk. Add the remaining sugar a little at a time, whisking until the whites will hold a stiff peak. Stir the gelatine into the cheese mixture, then add the whipped cream and whisked egg whites and fold together with a large metal spoon or spatula. Fold in half of the blueberries.

Turn into the prepared cake tin and cover. Refrigerate for at least 2 hours or until set.

To make the glaze, put 1 tbsp of the water in a small cup and the remainder in a saucepan. Add the sugar to the pan and bring to the boil, stirring to dissolve the sugar. Boil to make a light syrup. Mix the arrowroot with the water in the cup, then stir into the boiling syrup and simmer until thickened. Allow to cool slightly.

Add the remaining blueberries to the glaze, and spoon the mixture over the top of the cheesecake. Allow the glaze to cool completely and set before removing the cheesecake from the tin.

Blueberry Cheesecake; Strawberries Romanoff (page 92).

Few recipes prove as useful to the home cook as the classic sponge cake, or basic Victoria sponge, as it is traditionally called. Made simply from butter, sugar, eggs and flour, the basic recipe can be flavoured with all manner of ingredients, from chocolate to fresh fruit, or it can be enriched with ground nuts, dried fruit and alcohol. The result can be baked into a moist cake or steamed into a delicious sponge pudding.

Sponge puddings are great family favourites. The classic sponge cake mixture can be used plain, or flavoured with cocoa powder, coffee, stem ginger, nuts or dried fruits, for example. Toppings can range from golden syrup and treacle, to jam and marmalade. Fresh soft fruits such as raspberries, blackcurrants and blackberries, as well as apples and my favourite rhubarb also make excellent toppings for a plain sponge mixture.

The frangipan sponge is a useful derivative of the classic sponge cake. It forms the basis of many popular cakes and pastries and is used to create delicate madeleines – baked in their traditional shell-indented trays. The sponge is made by replacing all or part of the flour in the basic recipe with ground almonds. The resulting sponge is, understandably, very rich which is why it is often incorporated into baked fruit flans and puddings.

In case you are wondering, yes I did take domestic science at school and yes, I do remember chasing lumps of margarine around a large bowl with a

Classic Sponge

wooden spoon in an attempt to make a Victoria sponge. Good cooks are, it seems, born out of sheer determination – I decided then that this cooking lark wasn't going to get the better of me!

Lumps of margarine apart, the classic sponge cake is made by the creaming technique, whereby soft butter and sugar are beaten together before the addition of eggs and self-raising flour. The recipe is easy to remember since the quantities of butter, sugar, eggs and flour used are nearly always equal, assuming that an egg weighs 50 g/2 oz.

Strictly speaking, a classic sponge cake is not a sponge at all. The true whisked sponge is light and open in texture; and it is the air whisked into the eggs and sugar that makes the sponge light. The classic sponge cake, on the other hand, gets its lightness from the air beaten into the soft butter and sugar as well as from the chemical action of self-raising flour. Essentially, it is the self-raising flour that develops the 'cakey' nature. If ever you have used the wrong flour for making shortcrust pastry, you will know what I mean.

Self-raising flour is plain flour to which baking powder is added. To understand how baking powder causes a cake to rise, it is helpful to see flour as a starchy powder that turns into a glutinous dough or batter when mixed with a liquid. Self-raising flour produces the same glutinous mixture, but trapped inside are thousands of baking powder particles which, in the presence of warmth and moisture, produce bubbles of carbon dioxide. These, in turn, expand in the heat of the oven.

Eggs provide the necessary moisture to turn the flour into a glutinous batter and at the same time activate the baking powder. Eggs also enrich the cake and help it to set as it rises in the oven. The air beaten into the butter and sugar is also trapped in the glutinous batter, with the carbon dioxide, and together they cause the cake to rise. The butter and sugar melt and become absorbed into a beautifully light, yet rich cake.

*Illustrated overleaf:
Dundee Cake;
Devil's Food Cake;
Madeleines;
Madeira Cake.*

Cake *to a sinful devil's food cake*

1

The finest cakes are made by hand, using a wooden spoon. Hand beating is made easier if the mixing bowl is held just below waist level, resting on a kitchen stool.

2

Butter makes for a richer, cleaner-tasting cake and is preferable to margarine.

3

Soften the butter briefly in a microwave oven, or stir in a bowl over a saucepan of boiling water, taking care not to melt it. No amount of beating will soften butter that is too cold and firm. Soft butter should be the consistency of loosely whipped cream.

4

The creamed butter and sugar mixture must be of a similar consistency to the beaten eggs so the two can be blended together evenly.

5

Over-beating the butter and sugar can cause the cake to sink in the middle. If using an electric mixer, avoid fast speeds. As a general rule, soft butter and sugar should be beaten for no longer than 3 minutes.

6

Free-range eggs make for a brighter, richer cake.

7

Eggs must be used at room temperature. Cold eggs will cause the butter to firm and, in turn, the mixture to curdle. If a mixture does curdle when the eggs are added, stir in a little of the flour from the recipe.

8

Excessive liquid added to a mixture can cause sinking.

9

Take care when adding the flour as over-mixing will toughen the cake and cause the top to peak. Over-mixing is a common fault if an electric mixer or food processor is used.

10

To prevent dried fruits from sinking in the cake, dust them with flour after washing and drying. It will also help if you start the baking in a slightly hotter oven, then lower the temperature.

11

Any sponge cake will improve in texture if kept in an airtight container for 1–2 days before cutting.

The gentle art of cake-making begins with an understanding of how to make a basic Madeira cake from a classic sponge cake mixture. Many cakes are based on this simple creaming method and once you have mastered it you will have the confidence to tackle other recipes.

MAKES A 1 KG/2 LB LOAF CAKE

175 g/6 oz soft butter, plus a little extra for greasing
175 g/6 oz caster sugar
3 eggs, at room temperature
finely grated zest of ¹/₂ lemon
175 g/6 oz self-raising flour, sifted

1 Preheat the oven to 160°C/ 325°F/gas 3. Lightly grease a 1 kg/2 lb loaf tin with soft butter, then line with greaseproof paper and set aside.

Madeira Cake

2 Place the soft butter and sugar in a mixing bowl. Stand the mixing bowl on a tea towel on the work surface and beat the butter with the sugar using a flat wooden spoon until pale and fluffy. Scrape the mixture from the sides of the bowl with a spatula to ensure it is thoroughly creamed. Alternatively use an electric mixer, taking care to avoid over-beating.

3 Break the eggs into a measuring jug and whisk them with a fork. Add the eggs to the creamed mixture a little at a time and beat until smooth. (If the mixture begins to separate, add a little of the flour and stir until even.) Add the lemon zest and fold in the flour.

4 Turn the mixture into the prepared loaf tin and spread level. Bake in the centre of the preheated oven for 1–1¼ hours or until a skewer inserted into the

centre comes away cleanly. The top of the cake should split revealing a yellow interior. Allow to cool in the tin.

Madeira cakes are best eaten the day after they are made.

VARIATIONS

Victoria Sandwich: Divide the mixture between two base-lined and greased 20 cm/8 inch straight-sided sandwich tins. Bake in the centre of a preheated oven at 180°C/350°F/gas 4 for about 30–35 minutes. Turn out onto a wire rack to cool. Sandwich the cakes with jam and dust with icing sugar or caster sugar.

Frangipan Sponge Mixture: Proceed as above, but use 125 g/4 oz each butter and sugar, and 2 eggs. Replace the lemon zest with ½ tsp almond essence, and the flour with 125 g/4 oz ground almonds. Use to make madeleines (below), baked fruit flans and puddings.

Any cake made with ground almonds will keep better than one simply made with flour.

Madeleines: Lightly grease a madeleine tray and dust with flour. Place a heaped teaspoon of frangipan mixture in each indentation and spread level. Bake near the top of a preheated oven at 190°C/375°F/gas 5 for 15–20 minutes or until well risen and golden. Cool on a wire rack, then dip the edge of each madeleine into melted chocolate to coat. Allow to set.

Gooseberry Tea Cake

SERVES 9–12

125 g/4 oz soft butter, plus a little
    extra for greasing
125 g/4 oz caster sugar
2 eggs, at room temperature, beaten
75 g/3 oz self-raising flour
3 tbsp ground almonds
1 pinch ground mace
finely grated zest of ½ orange
125 g/4 oz gooseberries, topped and
    tailed

Topping (optional):
50 g/2 oz blanched almonds,
    chopped

If fresh gooseberries are not available use bottled ones, or try fresh apricots, redcurrants or cherries.

———————— ◆ ————————

Preheat the oven to 180°C/350°F/gas 4. Lightly grease a 1 kg/2 lb loaf tin with soft butter and line with greaseproof paper.

Place the soft butter and sugar in a mixing bowl and beat together until pale and fluffy. Gradually add the eggs and beat until smooth. Sift the flour, ground almonds and mace together into the bowl, add the finely grated orange zest and stir together. Fold in the gooseberries.

Turn into the prepared loaf tin and sprinkle with almonds if desired. Bake in the centre of the preheated oven for 50–55 minutes or until well risen and golden and a skewer inserted into the middle will come away cleanly. Allow to cool in the tin.

Rich Fig and Walnut Tea Cake; Gooseberry Tea Cake.

Rich Fig and Walnut Tea Cake

SERVES 9–12

150 g/5 oz soft butter, plus a little
    extra for greasing
125 g/4 oz dried figs, roughly
    chopped
1 tea bag
200 ml/7 fl oz boiling water
½ tsp orange-flower water (optional)
150 g/5 oz soft brown sugar
2 eggs, at room temperature, beaten
150 g/5 oz self-raising flour, sifted
50 g/2 oz shelled walnuts, ground
finely grated zest of 1 orange

For this recipe I have moistened dried figs in tea flavoured with a hint of orange before mixing them into a basic sponge enriched with ground walnuts. The cake is deliciously moist and improves with keeping for 1–2 days.

———————— ◆ ————————

Preheat the oven to 180°C/350°F/gas 4. Lightly grease an 18 cm/7 inch round cake tin with soft butter and line with greaseproof paper.

Place the figs and the tea bag in a bowl, pour over the boiling water and add the orange-flower water, if using. Leave to stand for 10–15 minutes.

Beat the soft butter and sugar together in another bowl until pale and fluffy. Add the eggs a little at a time and beat until smooth. Stir in the flour, ground walnuts and orange zest. Drain the figs and fold into the mixture.

Turn the mixture into the prepared cake tin and bake in the preheated oven for 1–1¼ hours or until a skewer inserted into the centre will come away cleanly. Allow to cool in the tin.

Farmhouse Fruit Cake

SERVES 9–12

150 g/5 oz soft butter, plus a little
  extra for greasing

150 g/5 oz soft brown sugar

2 eggs, at room temperature, beaten

175 g/6 oz self-raising flour

1 tsp ground mixed spice

150 g/5 oz sultanas, washed

50 g/2 oz seedless raisins, washed

50 g/2 oz mixed peel, chopped

50 g/2 oz glacé cherries (optional)

The traditional farmhouse fruit cake is a great family favourite. It is best allowed to mature for 1–2 days before eating.

————— ◆ —————

Preheat the oven to 180°C/350°F/gas 4. Lightly grease an 18 cm/7 inch round cake tin with soft butter and line with greaseproof paper.

Put the soft butter and brown sugar into a mixing bowl and beat together until pale and fluffy. Add the eggs a little at a time and beat until smooth. (If the mixture separates, add a little of the flour.) Sift half of the flour and the spice over the mixture and fold in. In a separate bowl, mix together the sultanas, raisins, peel and glacé cherries, if using. Sift the remaining flour over the fruit, and toss to coat evenly, then stir into the mixture.

Turn into the prepared cake tin and bake in the centre of the preheated oven for $1^1/_4$-$1^1/_2$ hours or until a skewer inserted in the centre of the cake comes away cleanly. Allow to cool in the tin.

Dundee Cake

SERVES 16

225 g/8 oz soft butter, plus a little
  extra for greasing

225 g/8 oz soft brown sugar

4 eggs, at room temperature, beaten

50 g/2 oz ground almonds

finely grated zest of 1 small orange

finely grated zest of 1 small lemon

225 g/8 oz seedless raisins, washed

225 g/8 oz sultanas, washed

200 g/7 oz self-raising flour, sifted

50 g/2 oz split blanched almonds

whisky or dark rum for soaking

The Dundee cake is becoming a familiar sight in many people's homes at Christmas time, in preference to the more traditional Christmas cake clad with its thick layer of hard white sugar icing. The main advantage of the Dundee cake is that it may be fed with alcohol right up until the day of eating.

————— ◆ —————

Preheat the oven to 180°C/350°F/gas 4. Lightly grease a 20 cm/8 inch round cake tin with soft butter and line with greaseproof paper.

Place the soft butter and sugar in a mixing bowl and beat together until pale and fluffy. Beat in the eggs a little at a time and beat until smooth. (If the mixture begins to separate, stir in a little of the flour.) Add the ground almonds and the orange and lemon zest. Toss the dried fruit in the flour and stir into the mixture. Turn into the prepared cake tin and spread level. Arrange the almonds on top of the cake.

Place the cake in the centre of the preheated oven and bake for 15 minutes, then reduce the heat to 170°C/325°F/gas 3 and bake for a further 2–2¼ hours or until a skewer inserted into the centre comes away cleanly. Allow to cool in the tin.

Store the Dundee cake in an airtight container for about 1 month before cutting, moistening the cake with whisky or dark rum to taste, from the underside, every 2–3 days.

Illustrated on page 98

Coffee and Walnut Marble Cake

WATCHPOINTS
◆
Classic Sponge Cake

SERVES 8–10

175 g/6 oz soft butter, plus a little extra for greasing

175 g/6 oz caster sugar

3 eggs, at room temperature, beaten

175 g/6 oz self-raising flour

50 g/2 oz shelled walnuts, finely ground

2 tbsp instant coffee granules

2 tbsp boiling water

Topping:

3 tbsp caster sugar

3 tbsp water

125 g/4 oz plain chocolate, broken into pieces

25 g/1 oz mixed chopped nuts

Dark coffee and rich walnuts find their moment of glory swirled into this beautifully moist marble cake, topped with chocolate icing and scattered with chopped nuts.

————— ◆ —————

Preheat the oven to 180°C/350°F/gas 4. Grease a 20 cm/8 inch angel cake tin with soft butter, dust with flour and set aside.

Beat the soft butter and sugar together in a mixing bowl until pale and fluffy. Gradually add the eggs and beat until smooth. Sift in the flour, add the walnuts and fold in evenly.

Transfer half of the mixture to a separate bowl. Dissolve the instant coffee granules in the boiling water. Allow to cool, then stir the coffee into half of the cake mixture.

Spoon the coffee and walnut mixtures alternately into the prepared cake tin and spread level. Bake in the centre of the preheated oven for 45–50 minutes or until a skewer inserted into the centre will come away cleanly. Allow to cool in the tin.

To prepare the topping, measure the sugar and water into a small saucepan and bring to a simmer, stirring to dissolve the sugar. Remove from the heat and stir in the chocolate until melted to a thick, shiny sauce.

Turn the marble cake out on to a wire rack, spoon the chocolate sauce over the top and spread evenly. Scatter mixed chopped nuts evenly over the surface. Allow the topping to set before serving, with tea or coffee. Marble cake should be stored in an airtight container, and will improve if kept for a day or so before eating.

Carrot and Hazelnut Spice Cake

SERVES 8–10

150 g/5 oz soft butter, plus a little
 extra for greasing
150 g/5 oz caster sugar
2 eggs, at room temperature, beaten
150 g/5 oz self-raising flour, sifted
1/2 tsp ground cinnamon
50 g/2 oz shelled hazelnuts, ground
175 g/6 oz carrots, peeled and
 coarsely grated

*Carrot and Hazelnut
Spice Cake;
Sticky Banana Cake
with Dark Chocolate
Chips.*

Whoever discovered that carrots could be baked into a deliciously moist cake must have been met with a certain amount of scepticism from those who for centuries had been eating carrots in savoury stews and soups!

————— ◆ —————

Preheat the oven to 180°C/350°F/gas 4. Lightly grease an 18 cm/7 inch round cake tin with soft butter and line with greaseproof paper.

Beat the soft butter and sugar together in a bowl until pale and fluffy. Gradually add the eggs and beat until smooth. (If the mixture begins to separate, stir in a little of the flour.) Combine the flour, cinnamon, hazelnuts and carrot, then fold into the mixture.

Turn into the prepared cake tin and bake in the centre of the preheated oven for 1 hour or until a skewer inserted into the centre comes away cleanly. Allow to cool in the tin.

Sticky Banana Cake with Dark Chocolate Chips

SERVES 8–10

125 g/4 oz soft butter, plus a little
 extra for greasing
150 g/5 oz soft brown sugar
2 eggs, at room temperature, beaten
3 medium-size ripe bananas, mashed
250 g/9 oz self-raising flour
1 pinch ground allspice
1 pinch salt
75 g/3 oz dark chocolate chips

There is only one thing better than a sticky banana cake and that is a sticky banana cake riddled with chocolate chips.

————— ◆ —————

Preheat the oven to 180°C/350°F/gas 4. Lightly grease a 1 kg/2 lb loaf tin or 18 cm/7 inch round cake tin with butter and line with greaseproof paper.

Beat the soft butter and sugar together in a bowl until pale and fluffy. Add the eggs a little at a time and beat until smooth. Add the mashed bananas. Sift the flour, allspice and salt together over the mixture, add the chocolate chips and fold in.

Turn the mixture into the prepared cake tin and bake in the centre of the preheated oven for 50 minutes to 1 hour or until a skewer inserted into the centre comes away cleanly. Allow to cool in the tin.

Store in an airtight container. The texture and flavour of this cake will improve if kept for a day or so before serving.

Chocolate Sponge Pudding

SERVES 4

Chocolate topping:

75 ml/3 fl oz single cream

1 tbsp caster sugar

175 g/6 oz best quality plain
    chocolate, roughly chopped

Sponge:

125 g/4 oz soft butter, plus a little
    extra for greasing

125 g/4 oz caster sugar

2 eggs, at room temperature, beaten

75 g/3 oz self-raising flour

25 g/1 oz cocoa powder

Sticky, spotty, gooey, dribbly, stodgy, steamy and dreamy – these are just a few of the words used by children and adults to describe their favourite sponge puddings. The basic mixture is a Victoria sponge, which can be flavoured with all kinds of ingredients. Toppings can be equally varied.

To get you going, here is a chocolate pudding with a dribbly sauce.

———— ◆ ————

To prepare the chocolate topping, measure the cream and sugar into a small saucepan and bring to the boil. Remove from the heat, add the chocolate and stir until melted.

Lightly grease a 750 ml/1½ pint pudding basin with soft butter and pour the chocolate topping into the bottom. Set aside.

To prepare the sponge, place the soft butter and sugar in a mixing bowl and beat until pale and fluffy. Add the eggs a little at a time and beat until smooth. (If the mixture begins to separate, add a little of the flour.) Sift the flour and cocoa powder over the mixture and fold in evenly.

Turn the mixture into the pudding basin and cover the surface of the mixture with a disc of greaseproof paper. Cover the entire basin with a piece of muslin 30.5 cm/12 inch square, or an old tea towel. Secure the muslin underneath the rim of the basin with string, then bring the opposite corners up over the top and tie into a granny knot. If you are feeling less traditional, the basin may be covered with kitchen foil.

To steam the pudding, stand the basin in a large saucepan, add 5–7.5 cm/2–3 inches of water and bring to the boil. Cover and steam for 1 hour, topping up the water as necessary. To serve, remove the muslin and the disc of greaseproof paper, run a table knife around the pudding and invert on to a serving dish.

VARIATIONS

For each of the following, make the sponge using 125 g/4 oz flour and omitting the cocoa powder.

Rhubarb and Ginger Sponge Pudding: To make the topping, mix 175 g/6 oz rhubarb, peeled and chopped, 3 tbsp stem ginger syrup and 25 g/1 oz chopped stem ginger.

Pineapple and Dark Rum Sponge Pudding: To make the topping, combine 3 fresh or canned pineapple rings, roughly chopped, 3 tbsp golden syrup and 2 tbsp dark rum.

Chocolate Sponge Pudding

Apple and Blackberry Sponge Pudding: To make the topping, put 225 g/8 oz Bramley apples, peeled, cored and roughly chopped, 50 g/2 oz blackberries and 1 tbsp caster sugar into an enamel or stainless steel saucepan, cover and simmer gently for 6–8 minutes until slightly softened.

Rich Chocolate and Almond Cake

WATCHPOINTS
◆
Classic Sponge Cake

SERVES 8
oil for greasing
1 recipe frangipan sponge mixture
    (page 101)
2 tbsp cocoa powder

Preheat the oven to 180°C/350°F/gas 4. Lightly oil a 450 g/1 lb loaf tin and line with greaseproof paper. Set aside.

Divide the frangipan mixture roughly in half, sift the cocoa powder over one portion and stir in evenly. Spoon the chocolate and almond mixtures alternately into the loaf tin and spread level.

Bake in the centre of the preheated oven for 50–55 minutes or until a skewer inserted into the centre will come away cleanly. Allow to cool in the tin, and store in an airtight container until ready to serve.

Illustrated on page 112

Devil's Food Cake

WATCHPOINTS
◆
Classic Sponge Cake ◆ Meringue

SERVES 8–10
150 g/5 oz soft butter or margarine,
    plus a little extra for greasing
5 tbsp water
225 g/8 oz caster sugar
75 g/3 oz plain chocolate, broken
    into pieces
3 eggs, at room temperature,
    separated
125 g/4 oz self-raising flour
50 g/2 oz cocoa powder

Filling and frosting:
575 ml/1 pint double cream
225 g/8 oz caster sugar
575 g/1¼ lb best quality plain
    chocolate, broken into pieces

The United States is home to the world's most wonderfully sinful chocolate cake. So rich and sticky is this offering that it has been designated devil's food. The method of preparation for a devil's food cake is a little different from a conventional creamed sponge cake, as the egg whites are whisked separately into a smooth meringue and folded in at the end. This luscious cake is sandwiched and frosted with an equally rich chocolate mixture.

———— ◆ ————

Preheat the oven to 180°C/350°F/gas 4. Grease two 23 cm/9 inch sponge tins, that are 5 cm/2 inches deep, and dust with flour.

Measure the water and 2 tbsp of the sugar into a small saucepan and bring to the boil, stirring to dissolve the sugar. Remove from the heat, add the chocolate and stir until melted. Leave to cool.

Beat the butter and 150 g/5 oz of the sugar together in a mixing bowl until pale and fluffy. Beat in the egg yolks. Sift the flour and cocoa over the creamed mixture and fold in gently, together with the melted chocolate. Whisk the egg whites in a clean bowl until they will hold their weight on the whisk. Add the remaining sugar a little at a time and continue whisking until stiff. Fold the meringue into the chocolate mixture, using a large metal spoon or spatula.

Turn the mixture into the prepared cake tins and bake in the centre of the preheated oven for 30–35 minutes. Allow to cool in the tins for 10–15 minutes, then turn out on to a wire rack to cool completely.

To prepare the chocolate filling and frosting, put the cream and sugar into a heavy saucepan and bring to the boil, stirring to dissolve the sugar. Remove from the heat, add the chocolate and stir until melted. Transfer to a metal bowl and leave to cool and firm, 1 1/2-2 hours.

To finish, sandwich the two cake layers with about a quarter of the filling. Swirl the remaining filling over the top and sides, using a palette knife.

Illustrated on page 98

Chocolate Angel Food Cake

WATCHPOINTS

◆

Classic Sponge Cake ◆ Meringue ◆ Whisked Sponge

SERVES 8

soft butter for greasing

5 egg whites, at room temperature

175 g/6 oz caster sugar

50 g/2 oz self-raising flour

25 g/1 oz ground almonds

25 g/1 oz cocoa powder

Chocolate glaze:

4 tbsp caster sugar

4 tbsp milk

175 g/6 oz best quality plain chocolate, broken into pieces

50 g/2 oz flaked almonds, toasted

Angel food cakes are renowned for their ability to combine richness with lightness. Although not a true Victoria sponge, the Angel cake is a classic sponge cake in the United States, and I have therefore included it in this section. One bite of this delicious cake and it is not difficult to see why it was given its heavenly name.

――――――― ◆ ―――――――

Lightly grease a 23 cm/9 inch angel cake tin with soft butter and dust lightly with flour. Preheat the oven to 180°C/350°F/gas 4.

Whisk the egg whites in a large clean mixing bowl until they will hold their weight on the whisk. Add 125 g/4 oz of the sugar a little at a time and continue whisking until stiff. Sift the 50 g/2 oz of sugar with the flour, almonds and cocoa powder on to a sheet of greaseproof paper, then sift again over the whisked egg whites and fold in with a large metal spoon.

Turn the mixture into the prepared cake tin and spread level. Bake in the centre of the preheated oven for about 45 minutes: the cake is cooked when well risen and firm to the touch. Leave to cool in the tin for 10–15 minutes, then turn out on to a wire rack to cool completely.

To prepare the chocolate glaze, measure the sugar and milk into a small saucepan and bring to the boil, stirring to dissolve the sugar. Remove from the heat, stir in the chocolate until melted and let stand for 5 minutes.

Place the cake on a serving plate and spoon the glaze over the top. Sprinkle with toasted flaked almonds and allow to set.

Apricot and Almond Sponge Cake

SERVES 8

soft butter or oil for greasing

225 g/8 oz fresh apricots, or
    400 g/14 oz canned apricot halves,
    drained

25 g/1 oz blanched almonds

Frangipan sponge:

125 g/4 oz soft butter

125 g/4 oz caster sugar

2 eggs, at room temperature, beaten

1 tbsp self-raising flour (optional)

½ tsp almond essence

125 g/4 oz ground almonds

To glaze:

4 tbsp apricot jam

1 tbsp water

Whenever fresh fruits are in season I like to incorporate them into a rich almond sponge cake. The fruits that work best tend to be those with stones, such as apricots, plums and greengages, although I have also had success with pears, fresh figs, gooseberries and redcurrants.

———————— ◆ ————————

Preheat the oven to 180°C/350°F/gas 4. Lightly grease an 18 cm/7 inch round cake tin with soft butter or oil, line the bottom with greaseproof paper and dust with flour.

Cut fresh apricots in half and remove the stones. Place an almond in each apricot half hollow. Arrange the fruit cut side down, on the bottom of the cake tin.

To prepare the sponge, place the soft butter and sugar in a mixing bowl and beat until pale and fluffy. Add the eggs a little at a time and beat until smooth. (If the mixture begins to separate, add 1 tablespoon flour.) Add the almond essence and ground almonds and fold in, using a large metal spoon. Spread the frangipan mixture evenly over the fruit.

Bake in the centre of the preheated oven for 50–55 minutes or until a skewer inserted into the centre will come away cleanly. Whilst the cake is still warm, run a table knife around the inside of the tin and turn out the cake on to a serving plate.

To glaze, measure the apricot jam and water into a saucepan and bring to a simmer, then brush over the entire surface of the cake.

VARIATION

If you want to substitute pears for the apricots, it is best to poach them first in a light syrup until tender. Fresh figs, gooseberries and redcurrants can be used just as they are.

Apricot and Almond Sponge Cake;
Rich Chocolate and Almond Cake (page 110)

'The discovery of a new dish does more for the happiness of mankind than the discovery of a star'

BRILLAT-SAVARIN

The success of the whisked sponge is founded on its ability to retain two of the most important elements in dessert-making: air and moisture. Its other redeeming feature has to do with simplicity: the recipe consists of three simple ingredients – eggs, sugar and flour – and these can be whisked ready for the oven in just five minutes. Unlike the classic sponge cake which forms the basis of plain and fruited cakes, the whisked sponge is used to create a variety of delicate cream-filled gâteaux, Swiss rolls and trifles.

The whisked sponge can be prepared in a number of different ways, some of which appear unnecessarily complicated. Some recipes require the yolks and whites of egg to be whisked separately and folded together, whilst others call for whole eggs to be whisked with a balloon whisk over a hot water bath. Both methods seem to me to require far too much time and effort for what amounts to a simple sponge. Providing that your eggs have not come directly out of the refrigerator, a perfectly adequate sponge can be made by whisking whole eggs and sugar together at room temperature, using an electric whisk. This I have found to be the easiest method.

To help you on your way to success, it is useful to have an understanding of how the ingredients behave before and after they go into the oven. Eggs and sugar are whisked into a thick foam, consisting of thousands and thousands of little bubbles of air trapped in the egg and sugar solution. Flour is then carefully folded in, so that each bubble is coated with starch which forms a

The ultimate light

Whisked

supporting structure. When the mixture is baked the bubbles expand and rise, creating a honeycomb effect.

Care must be taken during baking. If the oven door is opened too soon and the temperature inside is allowed to fall, the hot air trapped inside the mixture will contract, causing the sponge to drop. So if you are a curious cook who can't resist opening the oven door to check on progress, it may be worth investing in an oven with a glass-fronted door!

Once you have mastered the basic whisked sponge, you may be encouraged to experiment. Replacing some of the flour with cocoa powder will result in a beautifully light chocolate sponge suitable for fresh cream gâteaux, chocolate marquise or a stunning truffle torte. By replacing some of the flour with ground almonds, hazelnuts or walnuts, the sponge is made very rich and moist – perfect for special occasions. A whisked sponge readily absorbs liquid, enabling it to be further enhanced with a liqueur or fruit-flavoured syrup.

A chocolate whisked sponge enriched with ground toasted hazelnuts or almonds, can be turned into an unforgettable Black Forest gâteau. I have never been to the Black Forest in Germany, but I understand that the interior of this beautiful forest, carpeted with pine needles, is dark and mysterious. The dark, moist chocolate sponge of the Black Forest gâteau is sandwiched with bitter black cherries, soaked in their native Kirsch, and combined with more cream than is perhaps good for us. To resemble the carpet of pine needles, the entire cake is covered with a generous layer of flaked chocolate.

To make a Swiss roll, the basic recipe for a whisked sponge can be adapted so that it will roll up without cracking. The secret is to reduce the amount of flour to a minimum, thus allowing the eggs and sugar to retain sufficient moisture. The result will roll as easily as a blanket. In fact, the preparation is often referred to as a 'blanket sponge'.

Illustrated overleaf: Truffle Torte; Strawberry Charlotte; Peach and Redcurrant Cream Gâteau.

Sponge *to a wickedly rich truffle torte*

1
Weigh ingredients carefully before commencing.

2
Equipment and utensils must be washed thoroughly with hot soapy water to remove all signs of grease before use.

3
Ensure that sugar is not contaminated with flour or other debris.

4
Eggs must be at room temperature. If they are cold, the egg and sugar mixture will take much longer to whisk firmly.

5
Free-range eggs make a richer, lighter sponge.

6
Use an electric mixer. It is not practical to whisk the eggs and sugar by hand.

7
It is not possible to over-whisk the eggs and sugar for a whisked sponge. If in doubt, give them an extra 3–4 minutes to be sure they have taken in as much air as possible.

8
When cooked, the sponge will turn out with the lining paper covering the underside. Leave this greaseproof paper on the sponge during cooling, to help retain moisture.

9
Whisked sponges slice more evenly if they are wrapped in foil or cling film and kept in an airtight container for 1–2 days. Use a serrated knife for easy slicing.

10
Whisked sponges freeze particularly well: wrap tightly in cling film and store in the freezer for up to 8 weeks. Allow to defrost at room temperature.

This basic recipe and technique can be adapted to make chocolate, coffee, almond, hazelnut and walnut sponges. It is worth mentioning again that whisked sponges freeze very well, and are therefore always useful for last-minute birthday cakes.

MAKES A 20 CM/8 INCH SPONGE
soft butter for greasing
3 eggs, size 2 or 3, at room
    temperature
75 g/3 oz caster sugar
75 g/3 oz plain flour
To finish:
strawberry jam or fresh fruit
    (raspberries, strawberries, sliced
    peaches, etc.)
150 ml/¼ pint double cream,
    whipped
caster or icing sugar for dusting

1 Preheat the oven to 190°C/ 375°F/gas 5. Thoroughly grease a 20 cm/8 inch cake tin, that is 5 cm/2 inches deep, with soft butter. Cut a disc of greaseproof paper to fit the bottom and dust the inside of the tin with flour.

2 Break the eggs into a mixing bowl, add the sugar and whisk with an electric whisk until the

MASTER·RECIPE

Whisked Sponge

mixture is thick enough to leave a lasting ribbon across the surface, about 3–4 minutes.

3 Sift the flour over the beaten eggs and fold in with a large metal spoon or spatula, making sure to reach the bottom of the bowl where pockets of flour often hide. Without delay, turn the mixture

into the prepared cake tin and bake in the centre of the preheated oven for 30–35 minutes or until the sponge has shrunk slightly from the sides of the tin and feels springy to the touch.

4 Turn the sponge out of the tin on to a wire rack and leave to cool upside down with the lining paper on.

5 Whisked sponges are at their best after a day's keeping, although they can be used as soon as they are cool. Slice horizontally into one or two layers and fill with jam and cream, or fresh fruit and whipped cream. Dust with caster sugar or icing sugar to serve.

VARIATIONS
Chocolate Whisked Sponge: Reduce the flour to 50 g/2 oz, and sift 25 g/1 oz cocoa powder with flour. Use for cream-filled chocolate sponge cakes, truffle torte and chocolate marquise.

Rich Chocolate Whisked Sponge: Reduce flour to 25 g/1 oz, and sift 25 g/1 oz ground almonds or hazelnuts and 25 g/1 oz cocoa powder with the flour. Use for Black Forest gâteau and other rich cakes.

Walnut Whisked Sponge: Reduce the flour to 25 g/1 oz and sift 50 g/2 oz ground walnuts with the flour. Use for layered sponge cakes sandwiched with cream.

Hazelnut and Cinnamon Whisked Sponge: Reduce the flour to 25 g/1 oz, and sift 50 g/2 oz toasted and ground hazelnuts and ½ tsp ground cinnamon with the flour. Use for moist layer cakes sandwiched with chocolate filling.

Almond Whisked Sponge: Reduce the flour to 25 g/1 oz, and sift 50 g/2 oz ground almonds with the flour. Use for fresh fruit layer cakes, especially with peaches and raspberries.

Sponge Fingers: Spoon the whisked sponge mixture into a large piping bag fitted with a 1 cm/½ inch plain nozzle. Pipe about twenty-five 10 cm/4 inch long fingers on to paper-lined baking trays. Dust the fingers with caster sugar and bake in the preheated oven for 12–15 minutes or until golden. Allow to cool and dry, then peel from the paper. If they are not quite dry, leave on a wire rack for 2–3 hours.

Roulade of Strawberries and Cream

SERVES 8

1 Swiss roll sponge (see below)
225 g/8 oz strawberries
275 ml/10 fl oz double cream
1 tbsp caster sugar
icing sugar for dusting

When fresh strawberries are in season and the cows are busy turning green pastures into cream, the least we can do is to make this sensational roulade.

———— ♦ ————

Hull the strawberries and cut into quarters. Loosely whip the double cream with the caster sugar. Place the sponge face down on a clean sheet of grease-proof paper and spread with the cream. Scatter the strawberries over the top and carefully roll up from a short end.

Dust with sifted icing sugar and chill until ready to serve.

Swiss Roll

SERVES 8

3 eggs, at room temperature
75 g/3 oz caster sugar
25 g/1 oz plain flour
25 g/1 oz cornflour

Filling:

1/2 recipe crème pâtissière
    (page 27), or crème diplomat
    (page 27), or 275 ml/10 fl oz
    double cream, whipped

Swiss roll sponges are often difficult to roll. Reducing the flour and using part cornflour enables the sponge to roll without cracking or splitting.

———— ♦ ————

Preheat the oven to 220°C/425°F/gas 7. Line a 33 × 23 cm (13 × 9 inch) baking tray with greaseproof paper.

Place the eggs and sugar in a mixing bowl and whisk until thick enough to leave a lasting ribbon across the surface, 3–4 minutes. Sift the flour and cornflour over the mixture and fold in with a large metal spoon. Without delay, turn the mixture into the baking tray and spread evenly, using a large palette knife. Bake near the top of the preheated oven for 10–12 minutes or until springy to the touch.

Spread a clean tea towel on a work surface. Turn sponge out on to the tea towel. Allow to cool, leaving sponge face down with lining paper attached.

Remove the lining paper and spread the filling over the sponge. Roll up from a short end, lifting the sponge carefully with the help of the tea towel.

VARIATION

Chocolate Swiss Roll: Reduce the flour to 3 tbsp, the cornflour to 2 tbsp, and sift 3 tbsp cocoa powder with the flour.

*Roulade of Strawberries
and Cream;
Swiss Roll.*

Black Forest Gâteau

SERVES 8
one 20 cm/8 inch rich chocolate
 whisked sponge (page 119)
75 g/3 oz caster sugar
200 ml/7 fl oz boiling water
2 tbsp Kirsch

Filling:
350 g/12 oz jar stoned black cherries
 in syrup
2 tbsp arrowroot
3 tbsp cold water
275 ml/10 fl oz double cream

To decorate:
200 g/7 oz best quality plain
 chocolate, grated
8 fresh cherries

This irresistible dark, moist chocolate gâteau is riddled with black cherries, Kirsch and whipped cream.

————————— ♦ —————————

To prepare the filling, drain the cherries, reserving 200 ml/7 fl oz of the syrup. Mix the arrowroot with the cold water. Bring the syrup to the boil in a saucepan, stir in the arrowroot and simmer to thicken. Stir in the cherries and allow to cool. Softly whip the cream.

Slice the sponge into three layers. Dissolve the caster sugar in the boiling water to make a syrup. Moisten the sponge layers with the syrup, then sprinkle with the Kirsch.

To assemble the gâteau, spread a layer of cream over the first sponge layer and top with half of the cherries. Sandwich the second layer in the same way. Position the final layer on top and cover the top and side of the cake with a thin layer of cream. Mask the entire cake with grated chocolate. Pipe eight blobs of cream around the top of the gâteau and decorate with cherries.

*Black Forest Gâteau;
Dark Chocolate and
Chestnut Roulade.*

SERVES 6–8
1 chocolate Swiss roll sponge
 (page 119)

Filling:
275 ml/10 fl oz whipping cream
1/2 tsp vanilla essence
125 g/4 oz canned sweetened
 chestnut purée

To decorate:
150 ml/5 fl oz whipping cream
6–8 pieces candied chestnut
 (*marrons glacés*)
caster sugar for dusting
6–8 strips candied angelica

Dark Chocolate and Chestnut Roulade

As an alternative to this roulade's delicious chestnut filling, try crème pâtissière flavoured with praline, crème diplomat or whipped cream flavoured with vanilla.

————————— ♦ —————————

To make the filling, softly whip the cream with the vanilla essence. Stir a little of the whipped cream into the chestnut purée, then carefully fold in the remainder.

Place the chocolate sponge face down on a clean sheet of greaseproof paper and spread the chestnut filling over the sponge. Roll up from a short end, lifting the sponge carefully with the help of the paper.

To decorate, spoon or pipe blobs of cream along the top of the roulade. Top with candied chestnut pieces rolled in caster sugar and angelica.

Peach and Raspberry Cream Gâteau

WATCHPOINTS
♦
Whisked Sponge

SERVES 8

one 20 cm/8 inch almond whisked
  sponge (page 119)
2 tbsp golden syrup
125 ml/4 fl oz boiling water
2 tbsp dark rum or Kirsch (optional)
275 ml/10 fl oz double cream
1 tbsp caster sugar
350 g/12 oz raspberries (fresh or
  frozen)
5 small fresh ripe peaches

To finish:
50 g/2 oz flaked almonds, toasted
4 tbsp apricot jam
1 tbsp water

The second best thing to do with soft summer fruits, after eating them just as they are, is to use them with softly whipped cream to sandwich a beautifully moist sponge cake. I have used peaches and raspberries, but you may substitute any number of fruits such as redcurrants, strawberries, blueberries and loganberries, or tropical fruits, such as mangoes, papayas or paw paws, bananas, pineapples and kiwi fruit.

———— ♦ ————

Slice the sponge into two layers. Dissolve the golden syrup in the boiling water and brush generously over the sponge layers. Sprinkle with dark rum or Kirsch, if using.

If using frozen raspberries, tip them on to absorbent kitchen paper to defrost and drain.

Softly whip the cream with the caster sugar. If you prefer to use skinned peaches, cover them with boiling water to loosen their skins, then drain and peel. Halve the peaches, stone and cut into slices.

To assemble the sponge cake, spread an even layer of cream over one layer and cover with half of the peaches and raspberries. Cover with the other sponge layer.

Cover the top and sides of the assembled cake with a thin layer of cream. Mask the sides with toasted flaked almonds and decorate the top with the remaining peaches and raspberries. If desired, pipe a cream border around the edge of the gâteau.

To glaze the fruit, put the apricot jam and water in a saucepan and bring to the boil, stirring, then brush evenly over the fruit. Chill before serving. This gâteau is best eaten the day it is made. If preparing ahead freeze the sponge and assemble 2–3 hours before serving.

VARIATION

Peach and Redcurrant Cream Gâteau: Replace the raspberries with fresh or frozen redcurrants. Arrange clusters of redcurrants around the edge of the gâteau. This is a particularly delicious combination of summer fruits.

Illustrated on page 117

Strawberry Charlotte

WATCHPOINTS

◆

Whisked Sponge ◆ Egg Custard ◆ Meringue

SERVES 6

4 eggs, at room temperature,
    separated

125 g/4 oz caster sugar

275 ml/10 fl oz milk

3 drops vanilla essence

1 tbsp powdered gelatine

2 tbsp cold water

350 g/12 oz fresh strawberries,
    hulled

275 ml/10 fl oz double cream, softly
    whipped

15 sponge fingers (page 119)

To glaze:

4 tbsp apricot jam (optional)

Of the many gadgets and pieces of baking equipment that find their way into my crowded kitchen cupboards, the charlotte mould is one that has earned its keep. I use it for baked soufflé puddings, summer puddings, rum babas and crème caramel as well as the usual hot apple charlottes and cold charlotte mousses such as this. For this recipe, a creamy mousse based on an egg custard is combined with fresh strawberries and set in a charlotte mould. The mousse is then turned out and decorated with sponge fingers and more strawberries.

———— ◆ ————

Place the egg yolks in a bowl with 50 g/2 oz of the sugar and 2 tbsp of the milk and stir together. Bring the remainder of the milk to the boil with the vanilla essence in a heavy saucepan. Stir into the egg mixture. Return to the saucepan and stir over a low heat until the custard will just coat the back of the spoon, about 1 minute: the consistency should be that of single cream. Strain the egg custard into a clean bowl to arrest the thickening process.

Sprinkle the gelatine into the cold water and leave to soften, then stir into the hot custard until dissolved. Cool until the custard is just beginning to set; this is best achieved by stirring over ice.

Save half of the strawberries for decoration. Cut half of what is left into quarters and crush the remainder to a pulp with the back of a spoon. Stir the pulp into the setting custard. Put the other strawberries to one side.

Whisk the egg whites until they will hold their weight on the whisk. Gradually add the remaining 50 g/2 oz sugar and continue whisking until soft peaks can be formed. Fold about half of the softly whipped cream into the setting custard followed by the meringue. Stir in the quartered strawberries. Turn into a 1.1 litre/2 pint charlotte mould and refrigerate for 1½-2 hours or until set.

When ready to finish, dip the charlotte mould into hot water for the count of 10 and turn out on to an attractive serving dish. If the mousse will not shift, try shaking the mould from side to side. Cover the sides of the charlotte with whipped cream and press on the sponge fingers. Decorate with whipped cream and sliced strawberries. To glaze, put the jam in a saucepan with the water, bring to a simmer, then brush over the strawberries.

Illustrated on page 116

Sherry Trifle

WATCHPOINTS

◆

Whisked Sponge ◆ Egg Custard

SERVES 8

one 20 cm/8 inch plain whisked
    sponge (page 119)
4 tbsp red jam
225 g/8 oz raspberries or redcurrants
    (fresh or frozen)

Syrup:

4 tbsp golden syrup
150 ml/5 fl oz boiling water
5 tbsp medium sherry

Custard:

575 ml/1 pint milk
3 drops vanilla essence
3 tbsp custard powder
3 egg yolks
2 tbsp caster sugar

Topping:

150 ml/5 fl oz double cream
50 g/2 oz flaked almonds, toasted

Slice the sponge into three layers and sandwich back together with jam. Cut into large cubes and scatter into the bottom of a trifle bowl, together with the raspberries and redcurrants, reserving a few for decoration.

To make the syrup, dissolve the golden syrup in the boiling water and pour over the sponge to moisten. Sprinkle on the sherry and set aside.

To make the custard, measure 3 tbsp of the milk into a bowl. Put the remainder in a heavy saucepan, add the vanilla essence and bring to the boil. Add the custard powder, egg yolks and sugar to the bowl and stir until smoothly blended. When the milk has come to the boil, stir into the custard mixture, then return to the saucepan and simmer gently to thicken, stirring constantly. Pour the custard over the sponge and leave to cool completely.

To finish, softly whip the cream and spread a thin layer over the surface of the trifle. Pipe on a decorative border. Sprinkle with toasted almonds and decorate with reserved fruit. Chill before serving.

Sherry Trifle;
Viennese Pancakes with
Soft Fruit Centres.

SERVES 6

1 recipe Swiss roll mixture
    (page 119)
450 g/1 lb mixed soft fruits such as
    strawberries, raspberries,
    redcurrants, blackcurrants,
    peaches or tropical fruits
1 recipe crème diplomat (page 27) or
    275 ml/10 fl oz double cream,
    whipped
icing sugar for dusting

Viennese Pancakes with Soft Fruit Centres

WATCHPOINTS

◆

Whisked Sponge ◆ Crème Pâtissière

These delicious sponge pancakes are folded over a mixture of soft berry fruits and cream, dusted with icing sugar and served as a dessert or pâtisserie.

———— ◆ ————

Preheat the oven to 220°C/425°F/gas 7. Line two 38 × 30 cm/15 × 12 inch baking sheets with greaseproof paper.

Spoon the sponge mixture into three heaps on each baking sheet and spread into six rounds, roughly 15 cm/6 inches in diameter. Bake in the preheated oven for 8–10 minutes or until springy to the touch.

Spread out a clean tea towel on the work surface. Turn the sponge rounds upside down on to the tea towel. Leave to cool.

Fold the fruits into the crème diplomat or cream. Divide between the sponge pancakes, fold over in half and dust with sifted icing sugar.

Truffle Torte

WATCHPOINTS

◆

Whisked Sponge

SERVES 8

one 20 cm/8 inch chocolate whisked
    sponge (page 119)

2 tbsp golden syrup

125 ml/4 fl oz boiling water

3 tbsp dark rum or whisky

Filling:

275 ml/10 fl oz double cream

125 g/4 oz caster sugar

275 g/10 oz best quality plain
    chocolate, broken into pieces

To finish:

50 g/2 oz macaroons, crushed

If one could describe chocolate cakes as one might fireworks, truffle torte would resemble the whole box of fireworks going off at the same time – dangerously exciting but leaving you with a taste for more! Wickedly rich truffle torte is for the serious chocolate enthusiast. Use the finest dark chocolate you can get – Menier, Lindt Extra Fine or Suchard Bittra for preference.

——————— ◆ ———————

To prepare the filling, put the cream and sugar in a heavy saucepan and bring to the boil. Remove from the heat, add the chocolate and stir until melted. Transfer to a bowl to cool.

    Cut sponge into three layers. Dissolve golden syrup in the boiling water. Brush each sponge layer liberally with syrup. Sprinkle with rum or whisky.

    When the filling is cold and firm, beat it until smooth and use to sandwich the sponge layers, saving enough filling for the top and sides. Cover the sides with a thin layer of the filling and mask with the crushed macaroons. Pipe the remaining filling over the top. Chill until required.

Illustrated on page 116

Chocolate Marquise

WATCHPOINTS

◆

Whisked Sponge ◆ Meringue

SERVES 8

one 20 cm/8 inch chocolate whisked
    sponge (page 119)

2 tbsp golden syrup

2 tbsp dark rum

Filling:

200 g/7 oz plain chocolate

3 egg whites, at room temperature

3 tbsp caster sugar

275 ml/10 fl oz double cream

To decorate:

200 g/7 oz plain cooking chocolate

icing sugar for dusting

For this irresistible dessert, a rum-soaked sponge, topped with a creamy chocolate mousse, nestles inside crisp layers of dark chocolate.

——————— ◆ ———————

Line a 20 cm/8 inch springform cake tin with greaseproof paper. Slice the sponge into two layers and place one layer in the bottom of the tin. Save the other layer for another occasion.

    Dissolve the golden syrup in 125 ml/4 fl oz boiling water and brush generously over the sponge layer in the tin. Sprinkle with the rum.

    To prepare the filling, place the chocolate in a bowl over a saucepan of hot water and stir until melted, then remove from the heat. Whisk the egg whites until they will hold their weight on the whisk. Add the sugar and continue whisking until the meringue is firm. Add the melted chocolate

Chocolate Marquise.

and fold in with a rubber spatula. Whip the cream softly and fold in to the mixture. Turn on to the sponge layer and chill for 1 hour.

To decorate the marquise, melt the chocolate in a bowl over a saucepan of hot water. Spread the melted chocolate on to a smooth work surface; marble is ideal, although formica will do. Release the marquise from the cake tin. Before the melted chocolate has a chance to set completely, scrape it into long strips using a wallpaper scraper or broad knife and wrap around the sides of the cake. Cover the top with overlapping thin layers, starting from the outside and working towards the centre. Dust with sifted icing sugar.

Note: Do not be tempted to use quality chocolate for this decoration: it will not set firmly enough. Use best-quality chocolate in the filling.

'O, blackberry tart, with berries as big as your thumb, purple and black, and thick with juice, and a crust to endear them that will go to cream in your mouth, and both passing down with such a taste that will make you close your eyes and wish you might live forever in the wideness of that rich moment.'

RICHARD LLEWELLYN

If you have never had much success with pastry, I suggest you forget those conflicting rules that you have collected over the years and get back to basics. In this section I shall endeavour to explain how pastry is made, how the ingredients work together and, most importantly, what to do when things don't work out. Do remember, however, that when it comes to making pastry, no amount of reading can replace the need to practice.

It is far better to be familiar with just one or two good pastry recipes than to be bothered with an endless succession of new ones. I manage with just four basic recipes. One is shortcrust, made with or without sugar, which I use for sweet and savoury pies, flans and quiches. I make a rich biscuit pastry for sweet flans, tarts and mince pies, and choux pastry for a variety of éclairs, profiteroles and choux buns.

For vol-au-vents, risen flan cases and fancy pastries I confess I use frozen puff pastry, since making it yourself requires more time, effort and patience than can be found in a normal busy day. Bought pastry can never taste as good as homemade, but it is always reliable. For other occasions, when I need to combine flavour with flakiness, I put together a rough puff pastry made with butter. Rough puff doesn't have the same lift as full puff pastry, but it is quick and easy to put together and makes the most delicious covering for sweet and savoury pies.

Faultless, crisp

Pastry

to sensational flans and pastry gâteaux

Choux Pastry

It is not very often that I come across a pastry that appears to be completely new, but when a friend of mine started telling me about 'chooks pastry' and how she used it to make cream puffs, éclairs and profiteroles, it took me a moment to realize that she was in fact referring to choux pastry. After much teasing, I promised I wouldn't tell anyone about it. Please forgive me – Chooks. Should there be any doubt, the 'ch' is soft and the 'x' is silent.

Choux pastry is actually more of a thick batter than a pastry. It doesn't need rolling out, resting or chilling, and the more you beat it and knock it about the better. It is relatively easy to make, and providing the ingredients are all weighed out carefully, there is little that can go wrong with the initial preparation. Problems with choux pastry, should they occur, have to do mainly with baking – usually trying to bake too much pastry at a time and not allowing sufficient time for it to dry and set.

Pastry Making Equipment

It is all too easy to burden ourselves with too many modern gadgets and utensils. Don't be cluttered with more advice than is necessary, and don't waste your time and money on what often amounts to kitchen clutter. Apart from refrigeration, there have been few inventions in recent years that serve us as well as the good old-fashioned wooden rolling pin. Some gadgets, such as electric mixers and food processors, have their uses, but I would advise you to avoid using them until you can make good pastry by hand. Mixing machines are only as good as the people who use them, and technology has yet to provide us with a machine that tells us when to switch it off.

Before making pastry, ensure that your rolling pin is straight and your work surface is flat. Treat yourself to a new rolling pin, if necessary. Buy the plainest, most expensive one you can find, preferably from a proper catering shop, and take it for a test drive on the shop counter. I find thin rolling pins the easiest to control, but it is a matter of personal taste.

Flat working surfaces are important. Wooden pastry boards are fine when new, but have a tendency to warp if they come into contact with damp or moisture. Fitted hardwood surfaces are ideal if you can afford them, but they do stain badly with general use. Marble is by far the best surface to work on since it is perfectly flat, cool and even. Real marble is, of course, an expensive luxury, but will last a lifetime. I use a beautiful piece of marble that was once the top of an old washstand. Do not be tempted to buy cheap plastic-based marble or off-cuts of marble that are too small to work on properly.

The Three Ingredients

Basic pastry is put together from three simple ingredients – flour, fat and a liquid. We need to know how these ingredients respond to each other. It is not enough to throw them together and hope for the best.

FLOUR

Flour may look like a white powder, but it is in fact a combination of starch and the protein gluten. When flour is mixed with water, the gluten combines the starch and water into the elastic dough we are familiar with. Flours differ in the amount of gluten they contain.

Strong flours have a high gluten content and are used mainly for yeast baking where extra strength is needed to contain the active yeast gases. Plain, or medium strength flours contain less gluten. These are used mainly for delicate cakes and pastries, in which too much gluten would over-develop elasticity and toughen the cake or pastry.

Resting pastry before rolling and baking is not just an old wives' tale to be ignored. After it has been mixed, stretched or rolled, pastry invariably needs time for the elasticity to relax. Pastry that is not allowed a proper resting time is inclined to shrink and toughen when baked. If pastry begins to resist the even pressure of a rolling pin, don't force it – just give it a rest. With most pastry I allow a minimum of 45 minutes, or an hour or more if time. As scones are mixed lightly, the gluten isn't stretched so resting is unnecessary. Bread doughs that have the hell beaten out of them during kneading require plenty of rest, but this conveniently happens during the time the bread takes to rise.

Certain types of dough and pastry contain no water at all. Without water, the gluten present in the flour is not activated and stretched; therefore, no resting is needed before baking. Shortbread is an example of this type of dough. *Pâte sucrée* or rich biscuit pastry is another. This pastry contains a higher proportion of fat compared to a shortcrust, and is sweetened with sugar. Eggs are used instead of water to bind the pastry. The result is a rich, light pastry that does not shrink or toughen.

FAT

Butter, margarine and lard are the most common fats used in pastry. It is the fat which lend a flakiness to pastry, making it light and crisp. Butter gives the best flavour to pastry, but if you prefer you can substitute margarine, or use half butter and half margarine. Lard is less popular than it used to be, largely because of its oily flavour, although it is often used in combination with butter or margarine to lend a special character to savoury pie crusts.

We are all too aware that fats are firm when cold and melt to a liquid when they become warm, yet when these same fats are hidden away inside a pastry dough, we are inclined to forget. However, if pastry is left in a warm kitchen for longer than is necessary and the fat inside is allowed to melt into a liquid, the pastry will become difficult to handle.

Once pastry has been taken out of the refrigerator into a warm kitchen, it must be handled quickly and efficiently before returning it to its cold environment, or baking it. If for some reason you are distracted whilst rolling, dust the pastry with flour, fold it over once or twice and slip it back into the fridge where it will be perfectly safe. During the warmer weather it is best to make pastry early in the morning when it is cool, or save it for a cooler day.

LIQUID

The consistency of a dough is dependent on the amount of liquid used. Now this may sound quite straightforward, but because some flours are more absorbent than others, the amount of liquid needed to make a consistent dough can vary even with the same brand of flour. This has to do with changes in humidity. Although variations are only small, liquid measurements for pastry can only be approximate.

As a rule if you are making a shortcrust pastry with the usual proportions of half fat to flour, the amount of water will be roughly half that of the fat.

When adding the liquid, it should be added all at once to allow an even mixing. If the liquid is added a little at a time, stirring in between, the dough will tend to become dry in places and require unnecessary mixing with more water, thus over-stretching the gluten. It is much easier to add extra flour to a dough that is too wet than to add more water to a dough that is too dry. It is also important to ensure that the liquid you are using is as cold as possible so as to retain the overall coolness of the pastry.

Illustrated overleaf: Lemon Chiffon Pie with Berry Fruits; Lindy's Skyscraper Cheesecake; Profiteroles with Caramel Sauce; Gâteau Paris-Brest.

WATCHPOINTS

1
Never attempt pastry if you are short of time or in a bad mood.

2
Pastry is best made early in the morning when it is cool.

3
The finest pastry is made by hand.

4
Weigh all ingredients, and make sure you understand the recipe before commencing.

5
During warm weather, butter and margarine should be used straight from the refrigerator.

6
In any pastry recipe, you can substitute wholemeal flour for half of the white flour. In this case, you may have to use more liquid.

RUBBING IN

7
Soft spreading margarines are not suitable for rubbing in. Choose block margarine or butter. Unsalted butter has a cleaner fresher flavour than many salted butters.

8
To avoid aching shoulders whilst rubbing in, position the bowl at just below waist level. If necessary stand the mixing bowl on a tea towel, on a kitchen stool.

9
Aim to incorporate as much air as possible, and to achieve an even distribution of fat through the flour.

10
Do not allow the fat to soften and become absorbed. Flour that has absorbed melted fat will not absorb water and form into a coherent dough. Such a dough is inclined to crumble and fall apart.

11
If for some reason the fat does begin to melt and feel oily, place in the refrigerator to chill and firm for 20–30 minutes.

12
Work speedily, especially in warm weather and if you are inclined to have warm hands.

13
If you are distracted whilst making pastry and have to leave the kitchen, place the mixing bowl in the refrigerator.

ADDING THE LIQUID

14
Liquids must be as cool as possible to retain the essential coolness of the pastry.

15
Liquids must be added all at once, never in dribs and drabs. It is better to add extra flour to a pastry that is too wet than to add extra water to one that is too dry.

16
Never knead a pastry. If using an electric mixer or food processor, avoid over-mixing.

RESTING

17
Pastries which have water added must be allowed to rest for at least 45 minutes before use. Pastry that is not allowed sufficient resting time is liable to toughen when baked.

18
When freezing uncooked pastry, remember to first allow resting time because pastry cannot rest during freezing.

Shortcrust Pastry

Shortcrust pastry is the most basic type of pastry and can be used for sweet as well as savoury pies, flans, tarts and turnovers. The basic recipe can be easily remembered as half fat to flour, with the amount of water half that of the fat.

MAKES 350 g/12 oz
225 g/8 oz plain flour
1 large pinch salt
100 g/4 oz cool butter or margarine
3–4 tbsp cold water

1 Sift the flour and salt into a large mixing bowl. Cut the butter or margarine into even-sized pieces and add to the flour. To rub the fat into the flour, reach the fingertips down the sides of the bowl, bringing them together. As they meet lift the hands out of the

bowl, running thumbs from little finger to index finger, breaking through any large lumps of fat. Lightness is incorporated by lifting the mixture out of the bowl and allowing it to fall through the air. Continue rubbing in until the mixture resembles fine fresh breadcrumbs and tiny pieces of fat are still visible.

2 Add the water all at once, sprinkling it evenly over the surface, and stir together with the blade of a table knife until it forms large lumps.

3 Press together firmly with the fingers to form an even dough that leaves the sides of the bowl clean.

Over-mixing should be avoided where possible. Turn the dough onto a floured surface and knead lightly. Cover the pastry with cling film and allow to rest in the refrigerator for 45–60 minutes before using.

VARIATION
Sweet Shortcrust Pastry: Omit salt and sift 4 tbsp caster sugar with flour.

Note that when a recipe in this book calls for a specific weight of pastry, the quantity refers to the total weight, not the amount of flour used.

Rough Puff Pastry

Rough puff pastry is much more straightforward to make than puff pastry, and although it cannot compete with full puff pastry in making beautifully risen vol-au-vents, layered mille feuilles and fancy biscuits, rough puff is more than adequate for flaky pie coverings, turnovers, mince pies and sausage rolls.

Rough puff pastry is prepared in a similar way to shortcrust pastry. The main difference is that instead of rubbing the fat into the flour in small pieces, the cool butter or margarine is retained in hazelnut-sized pieces and incorporated into an even dough.

The flakiness of rough puff pastry is achieved by rolling the pastry out into a rectangle so as to flatten the pieces of firm fat into what amounts to a series of overlapping puddles, each interleaved with a layer of dough. As the pastry is folded neatly and rolled again and again, the layers of fat increase and the characteristic structure of the rough puff pastry is formed.

MAKES 450 g/1 lb
250 g/9 oz plain flour
1 generous pinch salt
175 g/6 oz cool butter or margarine
125 ml/4 fl oz cold water

1 Sift the flour and salt together into a large mixing bowl. Cut the butter or margarine into even pieces roughly the size of a hazelnut and toss lightly in the flour.

2 Add all of the water and stir into an even dough with a table

knife, taking care not to mutilate the pieces of fat. Turn the dough onto a floured surface and knead lightly. Wrap in cling film and rest in the refrigerator for 30 minutes.

3 Dust the pastry with flour and roll out into a long rectangle. Fold the pastry into three as if it were a business letter and turn it so that the two open ends are north and south. Dust with flour and repeat three times. Wrap the pastry in cling film and allow to rest in the refrigerator for 30 minutes before baking.

VARIATIONS
Rough puff pastry can be made with half wholemeal and half plain flour. If you wish to cut down on butter but retain some of the flavour, use half butter and half block margarine.

Rich Biscuit Pastry

Rich biscuit pastry has the advantage that it does not require lengthy resting times: it can be rolled out and baked as soon as it is made. Rich biscuit pastry has many applications although it is most widely used for sweet flans and tarts and coverings for fruit pies. The baked crust is less inclined to become soggy than shortcrust when in contact with moist fruit and soft fillings.

The secret of rich biscuit pastry is that, unlike shortcrust and rough puff pastry, no water is used in the recipe. The result is a short, non elastic pastry that handles as easily as plasticine. The short nature of the pastry is determined by the high proportion of fat.

Rich biscuit pastry is best used when the fat is cool and plastic. If, however, the pastry is allowed to firm too much in the refrigerator, rolling may be difficult. If you find that the pastry is too hard to roll, simply beat it firmly with a rolling pin before use.

MAKES 350 g/12 oz
200 g/7 oz plain flour
125 g/4 oz cool unsalted butter or
    margarine
50 g/2 oz caster sugar
1 egg, size 3 or 4

1 Sift the flour into a large mixing bowl. Cut the firm butter or margarine into even-sized pieces and add to the flour followed by the caster sugar.

2 Rub the fat into the flour between the fingers until the mixture resembles large fresh breadcrumbs. (If you are using an electric food mixer or a food processor, take care not to over-do the rubbing in.)

3 Add the egg and combine into an even dough. Although it is not essential for rich biscuit pastry to rest, in warm weather it may be necessary to firm the pastry in the refrigerator for 20–30 minutes before using.

VARIATION
Failed rich biscuit pastry can be turned into the most delicious crumble topping. Simply add 100 g/4 oz of rolled oats to the disaster pastry and rub together evenly. Spread the topping over a combination of fresh fruit sweetened with sugar and bake in a moderate oven for 35–40 minutes.

WATCHPOINTS

ROLLING OUT PASTRY

Ensure that your rolling pin is straight and your work surface is flat before you begin.

Do not allow the pastry to stick to the work surface or it will not roll out evenly.

Small pieces of pastry are more manageable to roll out than ones that are very large.

Pastry will only roll into a circle if it starts off as a neat round.

Pastry that is rolled out too thinly is difficult to handle.

Never pick up pastry by the edges. Use the entire surface of a hand or a rolling pin.

7

Never leave rolled-out pastry for long in a warm kitchen.

BAKING

8

Always start baking in a hot oven; if necessary, the temperature can be lowered after a while to dry the pastry.

Rolling out pastry

1 Dust the work surface and pastry lightly but evenly with sifted flour. Shape your pastry into a

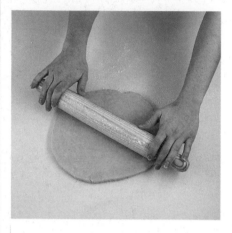

neat round, squash flat and roll out to a generous thickness, to the required shape.

2 As you are rolling ensure periodically that the pastry will move freely on the work surface. Work quickly and efficiently to retain the coolness of the pastry and use immediately.

Lining a Flan Tin

When lining a flan tin, the aim is to lay the pastry in the tin without stretching it. Metal flan rings are most convenient to use as they conduct heat particularly well, allow for a good depth of filling and can easily be removed after baking.

Loose-bottomed metal flan tins are also good. Glazed earthenware and porcelain dishes are poor conductors of heat and are often the cause of a soggy bottom. Allow a little extra baking time if you have to use one of these.

Allow 350 g/12 oz pastry to line a 20–23 cm/8–9 inch flan tin.

1 If using a flan ring, place it on a baking sheet. Roll out the pastry into a circle 10 cm/4 inches larger than the flan ring or tin.

2 To avoid stretching the pastry unnecessarily, lift the edges of the pastry towards the centre and push into the corners, turning the tin as you go. Press the pastry gently but firmly against the sides.

3 Firmly roll the rolling pin over the top of the tin to remove excess pastry from the edge.

4 To prevent the base of the pastry case from rising in the oven, prick it several times with a table fork. If using shortcrust or flaky

pastry, allow to rest in the refrigerator for 45–60 minutes before baking to prevent shrinking.

Baking Blind

Baking blind is the term used to describe baking a pastry case before filling it. To prevent the side of the pastry case from collapsing and the base from rising the pastry is covered with a circle of greaseproof paper and weighed down with dried beans or rice. Rich biscuit pastry is particularly suitable for baking blind because it dries more successfully than other pastries.

1 Cut a circle of greaseproof paper to fit in the pastry case and half fill with dried beans or rice. Bake in

the centre of a preheated 200°C/ 400°F/gas 6 oven for 15–20 minutes.

2 Lift out the paper together with the beans or rice. If the pastry base appears not to be dried out sufficiently, return the pastry case to

the bottom shelf of the oven to bake for a further 5–10 minutes.

Allow to cool on a wire rack. Store in an airtight container and use within 2–3 days.

Glazing

It is not absolutely essential to glaze pastry but it does improve its appearance when baked.

Beaten egg produces the most attractive glaze, although milk, or a mixture of milk and egg may be used. For an extra shiny glaze, add a

good pinch of salt to a beaten egg and stir until dissolved.

Brush the glaze lightly and evenly over the pastry, using a pastry brush. If you are applying pastry decorations, glaze these too.

Sweet shortcrust and flaky pastry may be glazed after baking by dusting with icing sugar and finishing under a hot grill.

Storing and Freezing Pastry

Pastry is best wrapped in cling film to be sure all air is excluded. It can be kept in the refrigerator for 2–3 days.

Uncooked pastry can be frozen successfully, and is best thawed and glazed before baking.

Apricot Custard Tart with Almonds

WATCHPOINTS
◆
Egg Custard ◆ Pastry

SERVES 6

1 recipe rich biscuit pastry (page 139)

50 g/2 oz ground almonds

900 g/2 lb apricots, halved and stoned

little caster sugar (optional)

Custard:

1 egg

1 tbsp caster sugar

2 drops almond essence

75 ml/3 fl oz single cream

When apricots are in season, try them baked in this delicious tart enriched with ground almonds and set with a smooth egg custard.

———— ◆ ————

Preheat the oven to 190°C/375°F/gas 5. Roll out the pastry on a floured work surface to a thickness of 6 mm/¼ inch and line a 23 cm/9 inch flan tin. Sprinkle the ground almonds over the pastry base and arrange the apricots, cut side down, on top. Bake in the preheated oven for 15–20 minutes.

Meanwhile, prepare the custard. Beat the egg with the sugar and almond essence and stir in the cream. Strain the custard over the apricots and bake for a further 10–15 minutes or until the custard has set. Serve warm or cold.

Bakewell Plum Tart

WATCHPOINTS
◆
Classic Sponge Cake ◆ Pastry

SERVES 6

1 recipe rich biscuit pastry (page 139)

225 g/8 oz dark plums

1 recipe frangipan sponge mixture (page 101)

In the town of Bakewell, in Derbyshire, you can still buy a Bakewell tart baked according to the original 19th-century recipe: a mixture of bread-crumbs, sugar, ground almonds and egg yolks spread over a layer of red jam in a pastry shell. I hope the inhabitants of Bakewell will forgive my version – a layer of plums covered with a rich almond frangipan decorated with strips of leftover pastry. Not quite the original but delicious all the same.

———— ◆ ————

Roll out the pastry on a lightly floured surface to a thickness of 3 mm/⅛ inch and use to line a 23 cm/9 inch metal flan tin, without stretching the pastry. Trim off the excess pastry and reserve.

Preheat the oven to 190°C/375°F/gas 5. Cut the plums in half and remove the stones. Scatter the plums over the bottom of the flan case. Cover with the frangipan and smooth evenly. Decorate with pastry strips cut from the trimmings. Bake in the preheated oven for 40–45 minutes or until a skewer inserted into the centre will come away cleanly. Serve warm or cold with vanilla ice cream or custard.

Bakewell Plum Tart;
Apricot Custard Tart
with Almonds.

Fresh Peaches in a Frangipane Flan

WATCHPOINTS

◆

Crème Pâtissière ◆ Pastry

SERVES 6

1 recipe sweet shortcrust pastry
  (page 137)

Frangipane filling:

275 ml/¹/₂ pint milk

¹/₂ vanilla pod, split open, or 2–3
  drops vanilla essence

3 egg yolks

2 tbsp caster sugar

4 tbsp plain flour

8 small macaroons, crushed

Topping:

6 ripe peaches, skinned

4 tbsp apricot jam, to glaze

A wonderful concoction – fresh peaches baked on a layer of frangipane cream – delicious vanilla-scented custard, riddled with crushed macaroons.

───────── ◆ ─────────

Roll out the pastry on a lightly floured work surface to a thickness of 3 mm/¹/₈ inch and use to line a 23 cm/9 inch flan tin. Rest in the refrigerator for 45 minutes.

To make the filling, put 2 tbsp of the milk in a bowl. Put the remainder of the milk in a heavy saucepan, add the vanilla pod or essence and bring to the boil. Add the egg yolks, sugar and flour to the milk in the bowl and stir until smooth. When the milk has come to the boil, pour it over the egg mixture, stirring. Return to the saucepan and simmer, stirring, for 3–4 minutes to thicken. Stir in the crushed macaroons, cover and set aside.

Preheat the oven to 190°C/375°F/gas 5. Line the flan case with greaseproof paper, fill with baking beans and bake blind for 25 minutes.

Spread the frangipane cream in the flan case, cover with the peach halves and bake for 35 minutes. To glaze, heat the apricot jam until melted and brush over the peaches. Serve warm or cold with a raspberry purée.

Fresh Peaches in a Frangipane Flan; Almond and Mincemeat Tart.

Almond and Mincemeat Tart

WATCHPOINTS

◆

Classic Sponge Cake ◆ Pastry

SERVES 6

1 recipe sweet shortcrust pastry
  (page 137)

200 g/7 oz mincemeat

1 recipe frangipan sponge mixture
  (page 101)

50 g/2 oz flaked almonds

icing sugar for dusting

A quick, easy and delicious way to use up leftover mincemeat after Christmas is to spread it in a pastry case, cover with a layer of frangipan sponge and bake to perfection. The result is beautifully moist and spicy.

───────── ◆ ─────────

Roll out the pastry on a lightly floured work surface to a thickness of 3 mm/¹/₈ inch and use to line a 23 cm/9 inch metal flan tin. Rest in the refrigerator for at least 45 minutes.

Preheat the oven to 190°C/375°F/gas 5. Spread the mincemeat over the bottom of the flan case. Cover with the frangipan and scatter over the almonds. Bake in the preheated oven for 35–40 minutes, or until a skewer inserted in the centre comes away cleanly. Dust with icing sugar to serve.

Lemon Chiffon Pie with Berry Fruits

WATCHPOINTS

◆

Pastry ◆ Meringue ◆ Egg Custard

SERVES 6

1 recipe rich biscuit pastry (page 139), or sweet shortcrust pastry (page 137)

2 tbsp strawberry or raspberry jam

200 ml/7 fl oz milk

3 eggs, at room temperature, separated

75 g/3 oz caster sugar

1 tbsp plain flour

finely grated zest and juice of 2 small lemons

2 tsp powdered gelatine

2 tbsp cold water

225 g/8 oz ripe berry fruits, such as strawberries, raspberries, blackcurrants, redcurrants, blackberries

To decorate:

ripe berry fruits, such as redcurrants, raspberries or strawberries

Lemon desserts are very popular for dinner parties providing, of course, they are not too sweet. For this old favourite I have replaced some of the sugar with seasonal berry fruits, which add both colour and flavour to this already delicious dessert.

———— ◆ ————

Preheat the oven to 200°C/400°F/gas 6. Roll out the pastry and use to line a 20 cm/8 inch loose-based flan tin. Line with a circle of greaseproof paper and dried beans, then bake blind for 20–30 minutes. Allow the flan case to cool completely.

Spread the jam evenly over the bottom of the pastry case with the back of a spoon and set aside.

Measure 2 tbsp of the milk into a mixing bowl. Pour the remainder into a heavy saucepan and bring to the boil. Add the egg yolks, 50 g/2 oz of the caster sugar and the flour to the milk in the mixing bowl. Add the lemon zest and juice and stir with a hand whisk until smooth. Pour the hot milk over the mixture and stir until even. Return to the saucepan and bring back to the boil, stirring constantly. Simmer for 1–2 minutes, stirring. Remove from the heat.

Sprinkle the powdered gelatine into a small cup containing the cold water, leave for a few minutes to soften, then stir into the hot lemon mixture until dissolved.

Whisk the egg whites in a clean bowl until they will hold their weight on the whisk. Add the remaining sugar a little at a time and continue whisking until stiff. Fold the egg whites into the warm lemon mixture using a large metal spoon or spatula. Fold in the berry fruits.

Turn into the flan case over the layer of jam, and spread out evenly. Allow to cool, then chill until the filling has set. Before serving, decorate the top with extra fruits.

Illustrated on page 134

Note: When berry fruits are out of season, use frozen ones or stoned bottled cherries instead.

Lindy's Skyscraper Cheesecake

WATCHPOINTS
— ♦ —
Pastry

SERVES 10–12

1 recipe rich biscuit pastry (page 139)

Filling:

700 g/1¹/₂ lb full fat soft cheese

225 ml/8 fl oz soured cream

150 g/5 oz caster sugar

1 tbsp plain flour

3 whole eggs

2 egg yolks

finely grated zest and juice of 1 orange

finely grated zest and juice of 1 lemon

1 tsp vanilla essence

To decorate:

strawberries

Hidden away in the heart of New York City is a family-run restaurant and coffee shop that has a well-earned reputation for an awe-inspiring cheesecake. Each slice stands as tall and as impressive as the glass-fronted buildings that ascend dizzily from the busy sidewalks of this city. While the original recipe for Lindy's cheesecake remains a closely guarded secret, there have been many attempts to recreate it elsewhere. Here is my version.

——————— ♦ ———————

Roll out a little over half of the pastry and use to line the bottom of a 20 cm/8 inch loose-bottomed cake tin. Shape the remainder of the pastry into a sausage, roll into a long strip and use to line the side of the tin. This is best done by cutting the strip of pastry into manageable lengths and overlapping piece by piece against the side of the tin. Place the lined tin in the refrigerator to rest the pastry while you make the filling. Preheat the oven to 220°C/425°F/gas 7.

Blend the soft cheese together with the soured cream, sugar, flour, eggs and egg yolks until smooth. Add the orange and lemon zest followed by the citrus juices and vanilla essence.

Turn the filling into the pastry-lined tin and bake in the preheated oven for 15 minutes. Lower the temperature to 140°C/275°F/gas 1 and bake for a further 1¹/₂–1³/₄ hours. The initial high temperature is necessary to ensure that the mixture rises sufficiently to gain lightness. Leave to cool completely in the tin.

To serve, carefully remove the cheesecake from the tin and transfer to a serving plate. Decorate the edge with a border of sliced strawberries. The cheesecake will keep for several days in a cool place; it does not freeze well.

Illustrated on page 134

Note: As this cheesecake cools it will shrink away slightly from the edges of the pastry case. The decorative strawberry border conveniently conceals the gap. The pastry case is very delicate, so take care when removing the cheesecake from the tin.

1

Weigh ingredients accurately before commencing.

2

Ordinary plain flour is quite adequate for choux pastry.

3

Choux pastry can be made just as well with an electric mixer or food processor as by hand.

4

Take care when boiling the water that none of the water boils away.

5

It is not essential that choux pastry batter is used and baked immediately. Shaped or unshaped batter will stand for 3 hours at room temperature before baking.

6

It is not advisable to bake choux pastry on greaseproof or non-stick paper as the paper will insulate the pastry from the direct heat of the lightly greased baking sheet.

7

If baking sheets are greased too liberally, the choux pastry will float across the baking sheet and gather in a corner.

8

It is not advisable to bake more than one tray of choux pastry at a time in a standard oven.

9

Do not open the oven door until the choux pastry has begun to colour.

10

Choux pastry isn't necessarily ready when it looks cooked. If you are not sure, take one piece out of the oven and see if it retains its shape. If in doubt, leave for an extra 10–15 minutes at a lower heat.

11

Larger pieces of choux pastry take longer to cook and often require lower temperatures towards the end to ensure proper drying.

12

Choux pastry is best eaten on the day it is made and should be filled just before serving, to retain crispness.

13

Cooked unfilled choux pastry freezes well, sealed in polythene bags, and will keep for up to 8 weeks. It should be crisped in a hot oven before use.

Choux pastry is easy to make. If you do not have 'the knack for pastry' then choux pastry is for you. It is made by stirring flour into a mixture of boiling water and melted butter. This enables the grains of flour to burst open so that the mixture will combine evenly with the eggs to form a smooth batter.

The batter for choux pastry contains approximately 60% moisture. When the batter is baked, most of this moisture is given off as steam which causes the choux pastry to puff up. As the choux pastry sets it reaches a maximum size. From then on the steam escapes through the outer shell.

The choux is cooked when all or most of the steam has escaped and the outer shell is crisp and dry. If it is taken out of the oven too soon, the steam inside will condense back into a liquid and render the outer shell soggy.

The secret, therefore, of good choux pastry is to allow sufficient time for the moisture in the batter to escape, thus enabling the choux to retain its proper shape when taken out of the oven. Choux pastry is used to make delicious éclairs, profiteroles, choux buns and gâteaux.

Choux Pastry

MAKES ONE QUANTITY
250 ml/9 fl oz water
75 g/3 oz butter, cut into even pieces
150 g/5 oz plain flour
3 eggs, size 2 or 3
1 pinch salt

1 Measure the water into a saucepan and add the butter. Place over a low heat and bring to a simmer.

In the meantime, measure the flour on to a piece of greaseproof paper and set aside. Break the eggs into a measuring jug, add the salt and whisk lightly with a fork.

2 When the water has come to the boil and the butter has melted, shoot the flour into the liquid all at

once. Stir over a steady heat until the mixture comes together into a coherent mass and leaves the sides of the saucepan.

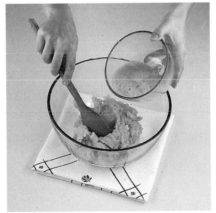

3 Transfer the mixture to a large mixing bowl and allow to cool for a minute or so, then add the beaten eggs a little at a time, beating the mixture either by hand or with

an electric mixer until even. Continue to add the eggs until the mixture reaches a smooth, stiff dropping consistency. The batter is now ready for use.

4 Preheat the oven to 200°C/400°F/gas 6. Lightly grease two baking sheets. For profiteroles spoon or pipe the choux pastry into little heaps on the prepared baking sheets, spacing two finger widths apart. For choux buns, spoon the pastry into larger mounds.

5 Bake in the preheated oven until crisp and golden brown, 25–30 minutes for profiteroles, 30–40 minutes for choux buns. Allow to cool on a wire rack. Fill as desired.

Ice Cream Profiteroles
with Hot Chocolate Sauce

WATCHPOINTS

◆

Choux Pastry

SERVES 6

soft butter for greasing

1 recipe choux pastry (page 149)

1 quantity vanilla ice cream (page 53)

Chocolate sauce:

150 ml/5 fl oz single cream or milk

1 tbsp caster sugar

175 g/6 oz best quality plain chocolate, chopped

Piping hot chocolate sauce poured slowly over a pile of profiteroles filled with vanilla ice cream, is the perfect finale to a successful meal.

──────── ◆ ────────

Preheat the oven to 200°C/400°F/gas 6. Lightly grease two large baking sheets.

Spoon or pipe the choux pastry batter into little heaps no bigger than a walnut in its shell, onto the baking sheets, spacing two finger widths apart. Bake one sheet at a time in the centre of the preheated oven for 25–30 minutes. Allow to cool on a wire rack.

Split each profiterole open and fill with vanilla ice cream. Place in the freezer until ready to serve.

To prepare the hot chocolate sauce, put the cream and caster sugar in a small saucepan and bring to the boil. Remove the pan from the heat, add the chocolate and stir until melted.

To serve, pile the profiteroles in a serving dish and pour over the hot chocolate sauce. Serve immediately

Chocolate Éclairs

WATCHPOINTS

◆

Choux Pastry ◆ Crème Pâtissière

MAKES 12

soft butter for greasing

1 recipe choux pastry (page 149)

1 recipe crème diplomat (page 27) or 275 ml/10 fl oz whipping cream, whipped

Chocolate topping:

4 tbsp caster sugar

3 tbsp water

175 g/6 oz best quality plain chocolate, chopped

Those of us who were not dreaming of cream cakes during French lessons at school will know that *un 'éclair* is a flash of lightning. Small boys must stop and wonder as they gaze into cake shop windows whether the word éclair is used to describe the speed at which these pastry fingers are baked or whether it has to do with the rate at which they may be eaten.

──────── ◆ ────────

Preheat the oven to 200°C/400°F/gas 6. Lightly grease two baking sheets and set aside.

Put the choux pastry into a piping bag fitted with a 2 cm/³/₄ inch plain nozzle.

Ice Cream Profiteroles with Hot Chocolate Sauce

Hold the piping bag as near parallel to the baking sheet as possible, resting the nozzle on your thumb. Pipe a length of about 10 cm/4 inches, as round as possible. Cut the end of the éclair by placing your index finger over the end of the nozzle. Pipe the éclairs six to a baking sheet, and bake one sheet at a time in the preheated oven for 30–40 minutes. Allow to cool on a wire rack.

To prepare the chocolate topping, measure the caster sugar and water into a small saucepan and bring to a simmer. Remove from the heat and stir in the chocolate until melted.

To fill the éclairs, split them open down one side and spoon or pipe the crème diplomat or whipped cream into each. Dip the top of the éclairs into the chocolate to coat and leave to set before serving.

Illustrated on page 153

Gâteau Saint Honoré

WATCHPOINTS

◆

Choux Pastry ◆ Crème Pâtissière ◆ Caramel

SERVES 8–10

225 g/8 oz frozen puff pastry, or
   rough puff pastry (page 138)
soft butter for greasing
1 recipe choux pastry (page 149)
1 recipe crème chiboust (page 27)
1 recipe caramel (page 69)
10 crystallized violets or rose petals
   (optional)

Only the French could have a patron saint of pastry-cooks and bakers; his name is Saint Honoré. This sumptuous gâteau was created by a group of Parisian pastry-cooks who, in honour of their patron saint, put together what amounts to a ring of choux pastry baked on a disc of puff pastry. The centre is filled with crème chiboust, and choux buns dipped in caramel are then stuck on to the ring like a crown. As you can imagine the gâteau does take some time to prepare but it looks spectacular.

———— ◆ ————

Roll out the puff pastry to a 6 mm/$\frac{1}{4}$ inch thickness and cut out a disc 20 cm/8 inches in diameter. Place on a baking sheet and pierce well with a fork. Leave to rest in the refrigerator for 45–50 minutes.

Preheat the oven to 200°C/400°F/gas 6. Lightly grease a second baking sheet and set aside.

Spoon the choux pastry batter into a piping bag fitted with a 2 cm/$\frac{3}{4}$ inch plain nozzle. Pipe the choux pastry on to the edge of the puff pastry disc to form a neat ring. Pipe the remainder of the choux pastry into 10 profiterole shapes no larger than a walnut on the second baking sheet.

Bake the pastries, one baking sheet at a time, in the centre of the pre-heated oven, 35 minutes for the base and 25–30 minutes for the choux buns. If the base is not quite cooked, lower the temperature to 180°C/350°F/gas 4 and bake for a further 10–15 minutes. Allow to cool on a wire rack.

Fill the centre of the pastry case with crème chiboust. Poke a hole in the side of each choux bun and, using a piping bag fitted with a 1 cm/$\frac{1}{2}$ inch plain nozzle, fill the buns with crème chiboust. Dip the tops of the choux buns into the caramel, and secure a crystallized violet or rose petal on to each, if desired. Dip the bases into the caramel and stick the buns on to the top of the choux pastry. Serve immediately.

Chocolate Eclairs; Gâteau Saint Honoré

Gâteau Paris-Brest

SERVES 6
soft butter for greasing
1 recipe choux pastry (page 149)
1 egg
1 pinch salt
25 g/1 oz flaked almonds
1 recipe almond crème pâtissière
   (page 27)
icing sugar for dusting

Once a year, the French stage a bicycle race from Paris to Brest, stretching some 600 km across the bumpy roads of Normandy and Brittany. True to form, an unknown pastry-cook at the turn of the century saw fit to create a circular cake in the shape of a bicycle wheel. A ring of choux pastry was sprinkled with chopped almonds, baked, split open and filled with a flavoured pastry cream. While legendary pastry-cooks rest in heaven, their creations live to see another day.

———— ◆ ————

Preheat the oven to 200°C/400°F/gas 6. Lightly grease a baking sheet with soft butter. Lightly grease a 23 cm/9 inch flan ring, place it on the baking sheet and set aside. (If you prefer to pipe or spoon the choux pastry free-hand, you won't need the flan ring.)

Spoon the choux pastry batter into a piping bag fitted with a 2 cm/³/₄ inch plain nozzle and pipe a single ring inside the flan ring. Pipe a second ring inside, adjacent to the first, then pipe a third on top. Beat the egg with the salt and brush over the pastry evenly. Sprinkle with the flaked almonds.

Bake in the centre of the preheated oven for 45–50 minutes. Make sure that the ring is sufficiently dry before taking it out of the oven. If in doubt, lower the temperature to 180°C/350°F/gas 4 and bake for a further 10–15 minutes. Allow to cool on a wire rack.

Slice the ring horizontally in half and remove any uncooked choux dough from inside. Sandwich back together with almond crème pâtissière. Dust with sifted icing sugar and serve.

Note that the unfilled choux pastry ring will keep in an airtight container for up to 3 days or it may be frozen until required. Crisp in a preheated hot oven at 200°C/400°F/gas 6 for 8–10 minutes before using.

Illustrated on page 135

VARIATION
Try Paris-Brest filled with crème diplomat, chocolate or praline crème pâtissière or sweetened whipped cream.

Dessert Biscuits

Crisp, light dessert biscuits are the perfect accompaniments to ices, sorbets and fresh fruit desserts. I have therefore included a few of my favourite ones to complement appropriate desserts. Both almond tuiles and brandy snaps can be set in basket shapes and filled with ice creams, sorbets and fruit confections.

Almond Tuiles

MAKES 24

50 g/2 oz butter, plus extra for
 greasing
125 g/4 oz icing sugar
2 egg whites
$\frac{1}{2}$ tsp almond essence
50 g/2 oz plain flour
50 g/2 oz flaked almonds, toasted

This biscuit takes its name from its resemblance to the curved roof tiles (*tuiles*) of the south of France. Almond tuiles are popular not only because they are deliciously light and crisp, but because they are both quick and easy to make. Traditionally, almond tuiles are served with ice creams and sorbets, although they may also be served as a petit four.

———————— ◆ ————————

Preheat the oven to 200°C/400°F/gas 6. Lightly grease two heavy baking sheets with butter and set aside.

Measure the butter into a mixing bowl set over a saucepan of boiling water and half melt, for no longer than 1 minute. Remove the bowl from the hot water and stir until the butter is the consistency of loosely whipped cream. Sift in the icing sugar and combine evenly. Add the egg whites one at a time, stirring until even. Add the almond essence, and stir in the flour to form a smooth batter.

Spoon the mixture into little heaps on the prepared baking sheets, six to each baking sheet. Sprinkle with flaked almonds. Bake, one sheet at a time, near the top of the oven for 5 minutes or until the biscuits are golden brown around the edges. Without delay, remove the biscuits from the baking sheet using a palette knife and set on the curved shape of a rolling pin.

When cool and set, carefully lift off the tuiles and store in an airtight container until ready to serve.

VARIATION

By spooning the mixture into larger heaps, the resulting bigger tuiles may be formed into basket shapes. Bake no more than three to a sheet. As soon as they are cooked, remove the tuiles from the baking sheet and mould each one over the base of an upturned glass. Leave until set.

Tuile baskets may be used to serve ice creams and sorbets.

Langues de Chat

MAKES 48
50 g/2 oz butter, plus extra for
   greasing
$^1/_2$ vanilla pod, or $^1/_2$ tsp vanilla
   essence
50 g/2 oz caster sugar
2 egg whites, at room temperature
50 g/2 oz plain flour

Langues de chat, or 'cat's tongues', are very popular served with ice creams and sorbets. They are at their best served straight from the oven, although they will keep for up to 2 weeks in an airtight container.

————— ◆ —————

Preheat the oven to 200°C/400°F/gas 6. Lightly grease two baking sheets with butter. Soften the butter and beat until it is the consistency of loosely whipped cream. Set aside.

Split the vanilla pod open and scrape out the black paste on to a wooden board. Add 1 tsp of the caster sugar and rub the paste evenly into the sugar with the side of a small knife. Add this, or the vanilla essence if using, together with the remaining sugar to the soft butter. Beat together with a wooden spoon until the mixture is light, 2–3 minutes. Add the egg whites a little at a time, beating well. Add the flour and mix to a smooth batter.

Spoon the mixture into a piping bag fitted with a 6 mm/$^1/_4$ inch plain nozzle. Pipe into 7.5 cm/3 inch lengths on the prepared baking sheets, keeping each length a finger's width apart. Bake on the top shelf of the pre-heated oven for 6–8 minutes or until golden brown at the edges. Transfer the biscuits to a wire rack whilst they are still warm and allow to cool.

Brandy Snaps

MAKES 36
50 g/2 oz butter, plus extra for
   greasing
125 g/4 oz caster sugar
50 g/2 oz golden syrup
50 g/2 oz plain flour
$^1/_2$ tsp ground ginger

Brandy snaps can be set into a variety of attractive shapes. Try setting them in individual tartlet tins to form baskets.

————— ◆ —————

Preheat the oven to 200°C/400°F/gas 6. Lightly grease two heavy baking sheets with butter.

Place the butter in a bowl over a pan of boiling water and half melt, no longer than 1 minute. Stir off the heat until the butter is the consistency of loosely whipped cream, then stir in the sugar and golden syrup. Sift the flour and ginger together and stir into the mixture to make a stiff paste.

Divide the paste into pieces no bigger than a grape, and bake three to a baking sheet in the preheated oven for 8–10 minutes or until golden brown and bubbly. Allow to cool on the baking sheets for a few seconds until beginning to set, then turn the biscuits over with a palette knife and roll each around the handle of a wooden spoon. Cool on a wire rack.

INDEX

———— ◆ ————